The End of Representative Politics

The End of Representative Politics

Simon Tormey

polity

The right of Simon Tormey to be identified as Author of this Work has been asserted in accordance with the UK Copyright, Designs and Patents Act 1988.

First published in 2015 by Polity Press

Polity Press
65 Bridge Street
Cambridge CB2 1UR, UK

Polity Press
350 Main Street
Malden, MA 02148, USA

ISBN-13: 978-0-7456-8195-5
ISBN-13: 978-0-7456-8196-2 (pb)

A catalogue record for this book is available from the British Library.

Library of Congress Cataloging-in-Publication Data

Tormey, Simon, 1963-
  The end of representative politics / Simon Tormey.
    pages cm
  Includes bibliographical references and index.
  ISBN 978-0-7456-8195-5 (hardback : alk. paper) -- ISBN 978-0-7456-8196-2
    (pbk. : alk. paper) 1. Representative government and representation. I. Title.
  JF1051.T66 2015
  321.8--dc23
                                                          2014030425

Typeset in 10.5/12 Sabon by
Servis Filmsetting Limited, Stockport, Cheshire
Printed and bound in the United Kingdom by Clays Ltd, St Ives plc

The publisher has used its best endeavours to ensure that the URLs for external websites referred to in this book are correct and active at the time of going to press. However, the publisher has no responsibility for the websites and can make no guarantee that a site will remain live or that the content is or will remain appropriate.

Every effort has been made to trace all copyright holders, but if any have been inadvertently overlooked the publisher will be pleased to include any necessary credits in any subsequent reprint or edition.

For further information on Polity, visit our website:
politybooks.com

CONTENTS

ACKNOWLEDGEMENTS

This book has its origins in a European Consortium for Political Research Joint Sessions workshop on 'Representation' held in Edinburgh in 2003. I gave what was even by my standards a rather leftfield paper, but it nonetheless provided me with an entrée to a world, albeit one I had little intention of inhabiting for very long. The paper was received with good humour and constructive criticism by those who were properly attuned to the intricacies of the topic: Gideon Baker, Henrik Bang, Michele Micheletti, Mike Saward, Graham Smith, amongst numerous others. I thank them for providing the initial stimulus that encouraged me to take up the issue in a more extended form.

As for the present, I feel very fortunate to work with a talented group of colleagues in the School of Social and Political Sciences at the University of Sydney. I would particularly like to thank John Keane, who has done so much to encourage discussion at Sydney of many of the key themes with which this work is concerned. I also acknowledge the important role locally of Pippa Norris, who, like John, has done a huge amount to enliven the environment for the study of representation, how it works and for whom.

I owe a great deal to the university for permitting me to take leave in 2013, when the bulk of the writing for this project was undertaken. During this year I offered a number of papers which became incorporated into the present work. I learned a lot from Wolfgang Merkel and colleagues at the WZB Berlin. I also thank the participants at a workshop on representation held at the Political Studies Association Annual Conference in Cardiff, particularly Mónica Brito Vieira, who provided detailed comments on my paper which gave much food for thought. I'm also grateful to the participants at a workshop on 'The Crisis of Democracy' held at Canberra University in 2014.

I'm very pleased to acknowledge the help of Ramón Feenstra of the University Jaume I, in Castellón, Spain. Ramón helped organize two periods of fieldwork which fed directly into Chapter 5 of the present work. He worked tirelessly for weeks setting up meetings, rounding up representatives and 'post-representatives' of political parties, taking me to all manner of events in Castellón, Barcelona and Valencia. Whilst in Spain we met with around a hundred activists. Quite simply, this would not have been the same book without their passion, engagement, knowledge and enthusiasm. Meeting individuals like these is the ultimate antidote to a certain weary fatalism that can creep into thinking about the present and future democracy. I salute them all, and thank them for their input into this work. *Muchas gracias!*

I'm also very pleased to acknowledge the direct help and assistance of Ben Moffitt, Andy Robinson and Ramón in reading and commenting on the full text of this work. All of them made me change my thinking or approach in some important way.

I'd like to acknowledge the help and guidance of the team at Polity Press, particularly Louise Knight and Pascal Porcheron. I am also grateful to the small army of colleagues behind the scenes who commented on my initial proposal and the final manuscript.

Finally (always finally), *gros bisous* to Véronique, and my children Maximilian, Gabrielle and Louis. Towards the end of the book I describe a form of democracy that is noisy, rumbustious and full of the clamour of unruly dissensus. Any resemblance to the family dinner table is entirely coincidental.

INTRODUCTION

There are not many truisms in the study of politics, but the view that representation is intrinsic to any system of democratic governance is probably one of them. Some people will speak and act on behalf of a group, political cause or identity and thus represent it; others will recognize themselves as being the object of this discourse and be represented by it. Some will hold power as representatives; other people will be represented. 'Speaking for others' and 'being spoken for' is, according to Hanna Pitkin, author of the classic work on the topic, *The Concept of Representation*, fundamental to understanding the dynamic of politics. As she puts it: 'In modern times, almost everyone wants to be governed by representatives . . . ; every political group or cause wants representation; every government claims to represent' (Pitkin 1972: 2).

Few readers of Pitkin's text would have had grounds for querying such an analysis when it first appeared in 1967. Now it appears increasingly problematic. The claim that almost everyone 'wants to be governed by representatives' is countered by a growing body of evidence that suggests that many of us have become – or are becoming – disillusioned with politics and politicians, with our representatives and with representation (Norris 1999; Dalton 2004; Hay 2007). Compared to the 1960s we vote less – when we vote at all. We are much less likely to join a political party, to be interested in the affairs of the state or the political class (unless it is in the context of a scandal). The citizens of advanced democracies trust politicians less than virtually any other professional grouping, including second-hand car salesmen. In response to such alarming indicators, the *Guardian* asked in a recent survey whether representative democracy was in 'terminal decline' (Burn-Murdoch 2012).

1

As for the second half of Pitkin's statement (*'every political group or cause wants representation'*), many emergent political groups and initiatives explicitly and implicitly disavow the inheritance of representative politics. Occupy, for example, like other recent movements, rejects the idea that it is seeking to represent, even as it proclaims 'We are the 99%.' We can put to one side for a moment the issue of whether and to what extent such responses achieve what they set out to do: avoid, query or move beyond representation. Of interest here is the discourse and repertoire of devices, manoeuvres and gestures groups use to distance themselves from 'representative politics'. In place of a politics based on a practice of speaking and acting for others, we now find a plethora of forms and styles of what might be called immediate or non-mediated politics: direct action, flash protests, Twitter-led mobilizations, pinging, hacking, squatting, boycotting, buy-cotting, occupying and other interventions of a direct, practical kind. Increasingly, politically engaged citizens don't vote, they act. They don't join mass parties contesting power; they create their own initiatives, 'micro-parties', networks, affinity groups, deliberative assemblies, participatory experiments. They don't wait for elections; they seek to make their views, anger, displeasure, known immediately, *now*. They don't read the media, they (to quote Indymedia) *are* the media.

Even those who are not particularly active politically share the activists' mistrust of politicians and the political class ('the Pollies', as they are unaffectionately known here in Australia). Many would, it seems, rather listen to the likes of Bono, Slavoj Žižek, Jeremy Clarkson, Zac de La Rocha, System of a Down, Russell Brand, Glenn Beck, Michael Moore – not least because they distance themselves from the world of 'politics' and 'politicians'. The fact that celebrities, some of them millionaires, can appear as authentic voices of a disenfranchised populace whilst living lives further removed from ordinary citizens than many politicians do is a sign of how desperate matters have become. So too is the success of anti-political or protest parties. Indeed, there seems to be an emerging correlation between the 'anti'-ness of a political party, its desire to distance itself from the political mainstream, and its popularity. The Tea Party is the classic example in contemporary politics. But the success of Beppe Grillo's Five Star Movement (5SM) in the Italian general election of 2013 is perhaps even more symptomatic of the self-contradictions of the age: a wealthy celebrity railing at the corruption and decadence of the political class as he lives out a life of relative luxury. Contemporary politics increasingly resounds with the sound of anti-political politics, anti-representational representation.

In view of these developments it should perhaps hardly be surprising that the issue of representation, what it is, how it works, from being a rather dowdy Cinderella topic, has become one of the issues – if not *the* issue – confronting political commentary today. After a period where representation seemed as a concept to be little discussed (no doubt partly owing to the excellence of Pitkin's work), a number of important texts appeared in swift succession to re-examine the evolving nature of representation: Bernard Manin's *The Principles of Representative Democracy* (1997), Nadia Urbinati's *Representative Democracy: Principles and Geneaology* (2006), Mónica Brito Vieira and David Runciman's *Representation* (2008) and Mike Saward's *The Representative Claim* (2010), to name but a few.

As well as texts focused on the concept of representation, an academic industry has sprung up examining the crisis of representation, with explanations and recommendations as to how to renew or regenerate representative politics. Many such texts rotate around the theme of tinkering with one or other aspect of the system of representation. Shouldn't electoral systems be more proportionate? Shouldn't we be encouraging more minorities or more women to take part? Shouldn't we have more assemblies, or different kinds of assembly or more opportunities to participate? As many experts have noted, young people are particularly unreceptive to electoral or mainstream politics. Shouldn't we be offering citizenship education in schools? Perhaps the answer is to follow the example of the Australians and the Belgians in making voting compulsory, thereby removing at a stroke one of the symptoms of our declining interest. There's a lively debate about public funding for political parties (Van Biezen 2004). If political parties are the locus of democratic life in representative systems, shouldn't we be doing more and spending more to make sure that they are able to function adequately? Shouldn't we be encouraging new political parties as well as established ones?

For others, however, the horse has already bolted the stable. The worried title of Donatella Della Porta's *Can Democracy Be Saved?* (2013) speaks for itself, as does Colin Hay's *Why We Hate Politics* (2007). As emerges in their analyses, we don't like politics and politicians, and wish a plague on their houses. More than this, we blame politicians for most of the ills that confront us, whether it be the impoverishment of public life or the sweeping tides of immigration accompanying globalization. Politicians have messed up our world, and now it's payback time. John Keane's *The Life and Death of Democracy* (2009), an elephantine history of democracy from Antiquity to the present, foregrounds the matter even more bluntly:

democracy appears to be 'dead', a victim of the growing incapacity of politics and politicians to engage with, let alone resolve, the key problems of our age. The best we can hope for is some sort of 'monitory' arrangement where those wielding power are made accountable through various ways and means to those subject to the whims of otherwise far-away politicians and technocrats. The *Guardian* was on the right lines it seems: terminal decline is a one-way street with the graveyard its final destination. We now live in 'post-democratic' or 'post-political' times. The idea of politics or, more precisely, democracy as a form of governance 'of the people, by the people, for the people' in the manner captured so brilliantly by Abraham Lincoln in the Gettysburg Address has withered in the glare of globalization, denationalization, public choice theory, neoliberalism, apathy and a multitude of other ailments.

What is to be done? Fixing up systems of representation so that they work better, so that they might be renewed, is the obvious place to start, one might think. Another is to rethink the basis of democratic life altogether. The shelves of our bookstores groan with all kinds of recommendations as to how to improve democracy through supplementing representation, or even replacing the representative component with some or other variant of direct or participatory democracy. The sheer variety of models on offer, from 'strong democracy' to 'associative democracy', through 'agonistic' or 'radical' democracy to 'deliberative democracy', is itself witness to the feeling shared by many that the existing paradigm for governing ourselves has become exhausted. Unless we reconstruct political institutions along lines that permit a much greater input into the political process by ordinary people, then the trend towards disengagement will continue. We, the people, will be cut adrift by the emerging technocracy.

Given the extraordinary lengths to which a multitude of expert commentators have gone to seek to resolve these matters, what can I possibly add that has not already been covered in detail somewhere else?

Perhaps it would help at this juncture if I offered an insight into why I think the dominant approaches have gone astray. My hunch is that those on the normative side of the question are on the right lines. The argument that representative styles or modes of politics offer a rather pale or thin basis for democracy is compelling. Critics are right to point out that defining democracy in such a way that it involves relatively few people acting on behalf of everyone else doesn't really get us to the kind of political community that Lincoln's eloquent definition seems to speak to – particularly democracy 'by' the people.

Our view of what democracy is – or rather what it might be – has become impoverished by the *practice* of democracy. It's therefore a worthwhile, some would say necessary, task for political theory to seek to show how democracy might otherwise be configured, and how what we have now might be improved.

Normative theorizing seems, however, to be less a panacea for the collapsing practices of representation than another domain in which the effects of the crisis of representation can be perceived. One of the ways in which the crisis plays out is in terms of the waning of what Jean-François Lyotard termed 'metanarratives' (Lyotard 1984: xxiv). These are stories or models of a just society, of a better world. Lyotard was referring principally to communism when he offered his analysis; but the argument extends to ambitious 'modernist' styles of theorizing more generally. Under contemporary conditions the idea of 'normative validity', of a kind of reasoning that offers us special insight into a more just, equal or democratic world, has lost its aura. Academics, political analysts, citizens, seem more sceptical about the claims of theory and the theoretical enterprise generally. Confidence in the wisdom and insight of intellectuals is at a low ebb, undermined no doubt by the propensity of many within academia and public life for pouring cold water on redemptive, emancipatory or normative schemas. Many of them were in any case a product of confidence in the direction and *telos* of modern society. As sociologists like Ulrich Beck and Zygmunt Bauman have long argued, this has been displaced by a preoccupation with complexity, risk and the increased sense of threat to the present as opposed to the possibility of creating better futures (Beck 1992; Bauman 1999). As Žižek memorably puts it, we seem to be living in 'the end of times', and 'endism' is not a fertile ground for the uptake of blueprints or promises of a better world to come (Žižek 2011).

This book is animated less by an explicit normative project than the suspicion that all is not quite right in the framing of this 'crisis', and in the prescriptions, whether normative or policy-focused, developed to address it. There's nothing at all wrong with normative theorizing, wishful thinking, utopianism or accounts of other or better worlds. But we should also be interested in the direction of travel implied in the trends and tendencies that are undermining processes of repre-sentation, that undermine 'politics' as this has been practised for the past two centuries – *including* normative theory, utopias and all the rest. It strikes me that the image of the decline and decomposition of politics that dominates contemporary commentary hides rather more than it reveals. In particular it seems to leave out a lot of what we should be calling politics, but which tends to get shunted into sidings called 'activism', 'protest' or 'mobilization' whilst we consider 'real' politics, the politics of the politicians, elections, political parties. But there's a lot of politics beyond this limited sphere. There's the politics of social movements, 'subterranean politics', the politics of indigenous peoples, the street, the politics of what Frances Fox Piven and Richard Cloward call 'poor people's movements' (Piven and Cloward 1988; Kaldor et al. 2012). There's the politics of and at the margin, at the periphery, a politics out of sight and out of mind except when it erupts televisually, spectacularly, dramatically. Much of this kind of politics lacks charismatic leaders, memorable slogans or watchwords. It might be routine or humdrum, a little initiative to combat an absurdly inappropriate development, as in my own neighbourhood, where residents have been fighting tooth and nail to ward off a hideously overblown project. But it might be something much more ambitious: combating climate change, challenging the corruption of elites, turning back consumerism, militarism, the march of the market.

Unofficial, non-mainstream, street politics is very much alive and kicking. Just thinking over the last couple of months whilst I have been plotting out this book: Hong Kong has been brought to a standstill by the mobilization of thousands of ordinary people. Brazilians have taken to the streets protesting against the bloated budgets for prestige projects and stadia. People have come out in their thousands in Turkey and in Bulgaria, hitherto regarded as safe 'consolidated democracies' where normal politics is supposed to work. There are on-going mobilizations of hundreds of thousands of people in Spain, Greece and Portugal confronted with the collapse of their standard of living. We could go on to mention the numerous insurrections, uprisings, stirrings, taking place currently in parts of China, North Africa, many parts of Latin America, India and Bangladesh.

Politics is not, however, just something to be found in far-flung corners of the world. There's nothing exotic about politics. One of the most striking features of the contemporary world is the readiness and facility of ordinary people to mobilize in defence of something or against some injustice. Crossing my own campus today, I was asked to sign a petition against Tony Abbott's proposed policy that would solve the 'boat problem' by placing refugees in camps in Papua New Guinea. There were stalls hosting various tendencies of revolutionary socialism. There was a group protesting against the use of non-fair trade coffee in the cafés on campus, and another seeking to recruit members to take action against climate change. University campuses are, of course, places where it is expected that we might encounter an enthusiasm for politics. Yet those familiar with the relevant literature will know that one of the persistent themes of work on the topic of the crisis of representation is the 'boredom' or 'apathy' of young people; code for the reluctance of the young to vote for or mandate a representative to act on their behalf.

Given the above, the claim that the contemporary world is marked by *depoliticization* needs to be properly contextualized so that it doesn't imply an absence of contestation, resistance, invention, experimentation, amongst ordinary citizens (Hay 2007). Clearly politics is going on here, there and quite possibly everywhere. I don't think we hate politics. We might hate one *kind* of politics, representative politics, the politics of 'the politicians'. But other kinds of politics, particularly politics that involves us directly as actors and participants, is, if anything, gaining force and momentum, as the examples above illustrate. Citizens are becoming less impressed by elite politics, less fearful of authority and the state, more inclined to act when they see an injustice or unfairness. However, political commentary tends to treat the *enacting* of politics as something marginal to the main business of politics. The media still concentrate on the politics of the politicians, on elections, on the events on Capitol Hill, in Westminster or Canberra. It is, after all, much easier to talk to select representatives than it is to swathes of anonymous individuals out in the street, on marches, manning the stalls and tables that gather signatures for a petition. On the other hand, given the waning interest and appeal of representative politics, it's easy to form the conclusion that politics is dying if all one is interested in is what happens on Capitol Hill, or how it is that our representatives are being received. To counter that impression one needs, as the saying goes, to get out more. Doing so might possibly give a different impression of politics. It might counter the view that something is draining away. Perhaps, on the contrary, politics is *filling up*?

But what does all this mean? Is the crisis in representative politics a temporary, contingent phenomenon brought about perhaps by the global financial crisis (GFC), or the decadence of the current crop of politicians? Or is there something happening at a deeper level which is undermining the representative function? If so, where is it heading? Should we be pessimistic or optimistic about the direction politics is taking?

I share the view of writers like Frank Ankersmit and Pierre Rosanvallon who are sceptical about the prospect of renewing representative politics (Ankersmit 2002; Rosanvallon 2008). I think they are right to cast doubt on the view that the crisis of representation is a contingent one, and by extension one that can be resolved with measures designed to take us back to where we were in the 1960s with mass interest and engagement with 'big party' democracy. I don't think the crisis can be blamed on the GFC, on the austerity measures that politicians have put in place to prop up ailing economies, on the shortcomings of financialized capitalism, on the peccadilloes or decadence of today's politicians. No doubt these contingent factors exacerbate the *sense* of crisis; but the decline of representative politics has its roots in something deeper and more difficult to negotiate: the on-going transformation of modernity, of political subjects, of the nature and form of our interactions with others. Something is changing in terms of the relationship between citizens and politics. The needs of political subjects are changing, as are the coordinates of political systems. Representative politics has increasingly the appearance of the political form of first modernity (Beck 1997), of nation states, of distinct homogeneous peoples, of sovereign territories and neatly assembled hierarchies of power and people. Contemporary developments are changing the coordinates of everyday life and in turn changing the nature of our attachments as political subjects.

Reflecting on the above, it is apposite to think through the implication latent in the work of those such as Rosanvallon, Ankersmit and Bang that we are seeing the waning of the aura of representation and representative politics. If we were to think of representative politics as a kind of paradigm, in a sense loosely related to Thomas Kuhn's use of the term (Kuhn 2012), then what becomes evident is that the paradigm is waning. This is a great worry for political analysts and those threatened by the ending of the paradigm: politicians, political parties, political scientists, who see the health of democracy as measured by our willingness to trust and respect our representatives to govern on our behalf. So much is clear, but if we were to contemplate matters in terms of a paradigm, this opens up a different vista – not just one of *loss*, but also one of *change* and *transformation* along new, perhaps unforeseen, lines.

Paradigm change is a painful business, but perhaps a necessary one as the condition of possibility for ushering in some mode of practice better fitting to the worldview, expectations, theorizing, practice, of the present and the future of present, as opposed to the past. I think we need to study and pay attention to what is being *created*, how it is that the political subjects are adapting to crisis, indeed *precipitating* crisis in the quest for something else, some new way of arranging ourselves and politics. But if the paradigm is changing, what is it changing to? Are we moving to some new variant of democracy: 'monitory democracy', 'post-democracy'? Perhaps, though I think Rosanvallon, Brito Vieira and Runciman and, indeed, Keane are closer to the mark when they describe contemporary developments in terms of 'post-representation' (Brito Vieira and Runciman 2008: 154; Keane 2009: 688; Rosanvallon 2011: 200). The 'post' here is a useful marker, that is, as indicating not the redundancy of the object in question, so much as its querying. This is, I think, a useful way of thinking the present conjuncture: less a passing of representation, and more an incipient problematization that evinces dissatisfaction but without presupposing the acceptance of a clear break or alternative.

Whilst it may be difficult to make out the exact nature of the 'after' of representative politics, certain themes are nonetheless emerging in the actions, prefigurations and demands of contemporary movements, citizen activism, modes and styles of organizing. The big picture is this: representative politics enacts what is sometimes termed a 'vertical' mode of politics. Someone at the 'top' represents those 'below' – speaks for them, acts for them and governs them. This in turn reflects the kind of societies out of which representative politics emerged. Early modern societies were deeply hierarchical: a small number of elites at the top, a 'mass' of individuals below, all held in place by a division of labour between those who owned and controlled the means of economic and social reproduction, and those who worked for them. The new emergent styles of politics are often 'horizontal', which is to say that they are often leaderless, 'bottom up' movements or initiatives that self-consciously avoid permanent or standing bureaucracies, offices and all the rest of the paraphernalia that goes with representational styles of politics. This, too, reflects some of the changes taking place in society, many of them promoted by the revolution in information and communications technology (ICT), which is having profound effects on the workplace, on the generation of news and media, on access to information, on styles and patterns of social interaction. Today's citizens are much more wary of representational devices and strategies of 'politics' and 'politicians'. The politically active want increasingly to be engaged, directly, now. They want greater control and transparency over the manner of their activism. That, too, is a symptom of larger social changes. These shifts provoke important considerations for normative theorists to take up: given the nature of global capitalism, which concentrates huge wealth and power in a small number of actors, how meaningful can 'horizontality' become in a world where powerful vested interests are seeking to maintain the status quo? Given a world of 'vertical' structures, political systems, economic opportunities, is the contemporary state deploying the concentrated use of force and power itself part of 'the problem' or part of the solution to breaking out of the old paradigm? One could go on.

As will already be apparent, trying to grapple with the nature of 'representative politics' is a Sisyphean task. It's a demanding concept, one that means different things to different people in different places. It's possibly even more slippery than the concept of democracy because it refers not just to how people are governed (by representatives), but, as Pitkin's commentary attests, to how we think about mobilization, the relationship between leaders and led, ideas and action. It is not just a matter of procedures or processes or institutions. We are also discussing relationships, understandings, roles, and our perceptions about who or what is in charge. It's a vexed topic. How to proceed?

The approach adopted is suggestive. It needs to be. We are looking for clues as to the nature of the crisis, an interpretation or reading as opposed to an explanation. Nevertheless, given what is at stake, we need to be bold and take some risks with a view to provoking further thought and reflection. We need to move from a position of acceptance of the necessity and inevitability of representation and representative politics to a more open stance that accepts that practices, discourses and procedures are located in a specific historical context. As that context changes, so we can expect changes in those practices. We also need to look at what people do and what they say in relation to the process and, importantly, how they enact other ways of relating to politics. A slippery business indeed. How does the book unfold?

The *first chapter* examines the contours of the crisis of representative politics, what it means, how it appears to experts. Political scientists have long been interested in the crisis of representative politics and chosen methods appropriate to their own understanding. What the relevant variables show is a decline in citizens' engagement with and interest in mainstream or electoral politics. So the image generated is one of *lack*. Something is ebbing away and causing a crisis. What is more difficult to capture in this approach is what is being created in its place, and how what is being created itself articulates with, and perhaps even causes, the decline to be explained. Yet as we noted above, many of today's mobilizations, initiatives and ways of doing politics seek to distance themselves discursively from representative politics and to enact another kind of politics. Paying attention to these kinds of initiative may give us some insight into the nature of the crisis. In particular it might help solve the puzzle alluded to above in Pitkin's comments. If at one level political representation is a 'given', then why do certain groups or movements seek to distance themselves from it? Clearly there's more at stake. Representation means something. It has certain connotations. It resonates in a particular way particularly at the margin – of politics, of society, of the geopolitical world where 'representative politics' was often plonked down amidst societies with quite different political cultures. If we want to understand the nature of the crisis, then it will be useful not just to look at a lack, but also to contextualize the efforts of those seeking to create some other way of doing politics.

The *second chapter* seeks to 'locate' representative politics. Implied in thinking representative politics as a paradigm is the idea that it is a specific practice operating under particular conditions in a particular time and place. As we know from Keane, Manin, Brito Vieira and Runciman, John Dunn, and a host of others, representative politics is a relatively recent phenomenon viewed from the perspective of the long march of political institutions and practices over the past millennia. The message we get from a work like Keane's *The Life and Death of Democracy* (2009) is that we should not be shy about treating representative politics and representative democracy as discrete objects of historical inquiry. The advantage of this approach over the more positivistically inclined approaches in political science is that it allows us to see that representative politics is a form of politics that arose in response to particular historical conditions. Of particular note is that the discourse of representation *preceded* the spread of democratic institutions and practices. Brito Vieira and Runciman suggest that we need to be attentive to the fact that it was an absolutist, Thomas Hobbes, who was amongst the first to articulate the virtues of representative politics over other ways of legitimating authority, and in particular the divine right of kings, which was the basis for Catholic rule in much of Europe (Brito Viera and Runciman 2008). By defining the sovereign as a representative as opposed to a ruler, Hobbes sought to alter the nature of the relationship between ruler and ruled, or at least our perception of it. This should alert us to an important aspect of representation: it is not the same as *democratic* politics. Representation stands in for or represents a disjuncture between those who govern and those who are governed. Where did that disjuncture come from? Who brought it into being? To what end?

In the *third chapter* we turn to explanations for the current crisis of representative politics. The dominant approach is to fix on temporary, contingent or short-term factors to explain the decline of interest in mainstream politics, seeking to find fault either with certain actors (politicians, citizens) or with the climate of opinion which has permitted neoliberalism, the market and New Public Management

11

theory to undermine the public interest, collectivism and democracy. Whilst each of these factors is certainly important in terms of getting to grips with the character of the present malaise, they are themselves *effects* as well as *causes* of crisis. In order to properly contextualize these factors, we need to examine the longer-term, structural changes to the nature of modern society, and in particular the impact of globalization, the collapse of collective identities and the emergence of individualization as a factor in determining the nature of political subjectivity and the attachments associated with it. What implications does this developing form of subjectivity have for politics?

In the *fourth chapter* we look at the decline of traditional styles of politics and in particular the political party. The decline of the political party is closely linked to individualization and the form of politics it gives rise to, which is less ideological, doctrinal and teleological. The inspiration for acting is often injustice, whether of a specific kind or one associated with a political system, a set of elites, corruption or incompetence. It is also linked to the decline of hierarchy and the division of labour, which underpinned organizational life in first modernity. As respect for and tolerance of hierarchy diminish, so contemporary subjects seek out flatter, more engaging ways of organizing, whether it be at work or in politics. Many of the more successful initiatives of recent decades have traded on their 'horizontal' character, offering the sense of being a participant as opposed to someone who will be represented. This transition to horizontal forms of organizing is greatly facilitated by developments in ICT and social media. Paul Mason documents this astonishing change in the capacity of ordinary people to intervene in the political field in his *Why It's Kicking Off Everywhere* (2012), an engaging first-hand account of many of these apparently spontaneous eruptions of political energy across the world. But how exactly is social technology transforming the nature of politics? What are the new modes of politics, the new ways in which people are organizing, mobilizing? Is the political party doomed?

Given the nature of the claims being made here it will be useful to see how such a transformation is taking place on the ground. In the *fifth chapter* I offer a commentary on the mobilization of the *Indignados*, which took place in Spain in 2011. The case study will help develop an understanding of certain developments in the political field. This is particularly the case with regards to political parties, up to now central to the functioning of representative democracies. Traditional political parties are, as already documented, under great strain to justify their centrality at the heart of democratic life when in terms of their own membership they are a declining force. The intriguing story from Spain is the recasting of the political party as a vehicle for protest movements, citizen platforms and all manner of activisms, some of them avowedly 'anti-party'. The importance of documenting this transformation at close hand is that it addresses one of the key puzzles in connection to the transition from representative to distributed, participatory and networked forms of politics. This is the articulation between the kinds of mobilizations facilitated by social media and the apparatus of governance. Social media, as is clear, are a fantastic means for organizing protests and initiatives, but can they be used to create more durable forms of mobilization? And what might the function of these emerging organizations be? Are they purely mechanisms of protest, or do they offer further clues as to the direction that democratic *governance* may take?

This leads us to the *sixth chapter*, where I seek to draw out the implications of the decline of representative politics by reference to the direction in which democracy may be heading given the developments we have been looking at. Even amongst those who accept that a fundamental transformation is taking place, the mood is pessimistic. We have already mentioned the work of John Keane, who has done much to prepare the ground for thinking about what lies ahead. Keane is at best ambivalent about contemporary developments, as the title of his *The Life and Death of Democracy* attests. If democracy is not already dead, then it is entering uncharted waters in the transition from a fully representative style of governance to 'monitory democracy' (Keane 2011). Pierre Rosanvallon puts a similar spin on contemporary developments, describing the proliferation of new forms of political mobilization as 'counter-democracy' (Rosanvallon 2008). He goes on to document the emergence of 'negative democracy', as if to reiterate the fact that the line of march is towards a dark place. Zygmunt Bauman, who has done so much to pave the way for thinking about the direction contemporary society is taking, can think of very few positives when he surveys the contemporary scene (Bauman 1999). All around us are perils, risks, pitfalls. Everywhere we find the clamour of consumerism, narcissism, individualism, 'anti-politics'.

Is the democratic glass really half-empty? Is it really the case that with the proliferation of political initiatives, with the multiplication of ways in which ordinary people can engage in politics, set initiatives in motion, create new groups and organizations with much greater facility than before, we should conclude that democracy is dead or dying? Perhaps we are getting the matter back to front? But if we are, then clearly we need some new concepts and new ways of relating to democracy itself. In particular we need a new language to describe how these initiatives relate to the political field, to governance and to the prospects for democracy itself. We may need to turn our sense of the political 'inside out'. It may be that we need to pursue Jacques Rancière's suggestion that we see the democratic component of contemporary existence as lying outside or beyond the apparatus of governance, or *Police*, as he puts it (Rancière 2010: 36). By recasting democracy as an activity engaging 'everyone and anyone', as opposed to something undertaken by our 'representatives', we may – by a perhaps strange quirk of historical fate – find ourselves writing about not the death of democracy, but rather its reinvigoration, albeit *after* representation.

— 1 —

CONTOURS OF A 'CRISIS'

Unusually for a topic in politics, there is broad agreement that there is a 'crisis of representation'– or if not a crisis, then something serious enough to make us want to think hard about what we can do to improve the quality of representation, representative bodies, representative practices. At some level there is always a crisis of representation or a crisis of democracy. It's in the DNA of democracies that there is a continual shortfall between what politicians promise and what they deliver, between what theorists of democracy think democracy should be like and how it turns out – leading to disappointment. Someone, somewhere has described representative politics as in crisis since at least the 1880s (Manin 1997; Rosanvallon 2011: 3). More unusual, however, is the shared perception of crisis across the ideological and methodological spectrum. It's not just political scientists or political theorists, or conservatives or liberals or Marxists who think there's a crisis of representation. It's virtually everyone with an opinion on the matter. What is equally true, however, is that not everyone means the same thing by 'the crisis of representation'. There is what we might term a politics of what we mean by 'crisis'. How one reads the crisis, or, better, *narrates* the crisis, has important consequences in terms of thinking about what to do about it. It will tell us a lot about what kind of action is needed to address the crisis to get 'politics' back on its feet – or alternatively to rethink politics 'after' representation.

So an important task is to explore the contours of the crisis. What I mean by this is the different ways in which the crisis is narrated and explored. Political scientists are keen on *measures* of 'crisis', and it will therefore be important to take stock of what they say. What are the signs or symptoms of crisis? What measures are relevant? What

15

are the conclusions drawn? But looking at graphs and data only paints one part of the story. It certainly tells us about what is lacking – and thus how the crisis cashes out in concrete terms as far in particular as elections are concerned. Yet politics hasn't gone away because there is a crisis of representation. Far from it. As I think is obvious, we are living in intensely *politicized* times. We are living through what Ulrich Beck terms the 'reinvention of politics' (Beck 1997). One of the stakes in this reinvention is the nature of representation itself – who represents whom, and how. So the crisis of representation is also provoked or created by the actions of movements and ordinary people who *contest* not only what representatives or politicians do in their name, but also the system that blocks access to power, influence, resources. So as well as looking at measures of 'crisis', it will be useful to examine the discourse of the crisis and how it is that activists and politicians adapt to crisis. Why do people reject representative politics? What do those engaging in politics say about themselves? How do they enact a politics 'after' representation if they do?

Contours of a crisis I: the view from above

For the most part, as we have seen, political commentary accepts that there is a crisis of representative politics. Nevertheless, many political scientists take comfort from the fact that representative democracy is at one level highly successful, so successful that it led Francis Fukuyama famously to proclaim that democracy had proved itself to be the highest form of political organization and thus that we could meaningfully evoke 'the end of history' (Fukuyama 1992). A majority of nation states have some form of representative democracy, albeit more or less 'consolidated', usually code for looking more for less like the United States of America. However, it is the line of travel that is important, less so the details of particular arrangements. The line of travel suggests that democracy in its representative form will continue to be the dominant or hegemonic political form for some time to come. This accepted, how does the crisis of representative politics manifest itself?

Surveying the vast literature on the topic, four variables stand out as particularly significant in how political scientists read the state of play: voter turnout, membership of political parties, trust in politicians and interest in mainstream electoral politics. Given that the material is well documented elsewhere, we can be brief (Hayward 1996; Norris 1999; Dalton 2002; Norris 2002; Dalton 2004; Hay 2007).

16

Voter turnout

Ultimately, the measure many commentators regard as key to gauging the health or otherwise of any given system of representation is whether ordinary people engage with it. The most direct measure of engagement on those terms is whether we turn out to vote. It's a simple and intuitively felt calculus at one level. The more people vote as a percentage of the population, the easier it is to draw the conclusion that the system is seen as legitimate by those who count, ordinary citizens. A declining turnout is, by contrast, often taken to indicate that something is wrong, and that therefore we ought to be worried about the relationship between citizens and the political system. So what do the numbers show?

Interestingly, the picture is mixed. If we just focus on presidential elections in presidential systems or on general elections in parliamentary ones, then it is at least debatable whether the term 'crisis' is really applicable. In the US, turnout for presidential elections looked as if it was in serious decline over the course of the 1970s and 1980s, but then recovered over the course of the 2000s to reach levels that would not have been out of place in the middle of the twentieth century, with around 60% of the population voting. The UK, along with other European countries, displays a more worrying trend in that turnout looks to have entered a pattern of decline from the 1960s with little to make commentators think that it will recover any time soon. Many European countries show a decline from around the 80 to 90% mark to 70 or 60% over the course of the last half-century. However, the picture is far from clear. Where electorates perceive the stakes of a given election to be high, they can turn out in greater numbers, as, for example, in the French presidential election of 2012, the German federal elections of 2013 and the Italian general election of the same year.

Around the rest of the world there seems to be a correlation between voter turnout and the moment when democratic elections are established. Often, the more recent the transition to democracy, the higher the turnout (Vietnam, Tunisia, Angola, East Timor, being examples). So the spread of representative democracy around the world isn't enough for many to offset the feeling that 'crisis' is looming, if not already with us. As democracies mature, so voter turnout seems to decline. But the correlation is far from automatic, and in any case disrupted by the effect of contingent events such as the GFC, which has boosted turnout as citizens perceive that there is more at stake in the electoral contest. Iceland, for example, recorded a turnout of over 85% in its 2009 elections, notwithstanding the fact that there were significant protests and demonstrations against the elites in the aftermath of national bankruptcy.

Moving away from the national level towards the *subnational*, on the one hand, and the *supranational*, on the other, the picture is gloomier. Across mature democracies voter turnouts for regional and local elections have shown a serious slump over the past four decades. It is now unexceptional to see voter turnout at the 20 or 30% mark. The same story is true at the level of the supranational, for example in EU elections. Citizens have increasingly turned their back on Euro elections, and where they haven't they have often cast a protest vote in favour of avowedly anti-European or anti-establishment parties, as in 2014, when anti-EU parties such as the UK Independence Party, or UKIP, scored large gains on a 30% turnout. Some constituencies in the UK have seen turnout drop to as low as 10% of the electorate, which, much to the amusement of sceptics, is on a par with the number of people voting in the Eurovision Song Contest or *The X Factor* (Burn-Murdoch and Rogers 2012).

If turnout was the only means by which we could establish the health or otherwise of representative politics, the jury might still be out on whether the epithet 'crisis' really applies. As seems clear, when voters perceive there is something important at stake, they will vote; if not, then they will stay away. General elections and presidential elections 'count'; elections for mayors, Euro-MPs, local politicians and all the rest count a lot less. In any case, analysis of voter turnout usually comes with a health warning. Political systems deploy a range of different modes of voting, each with its own incentives and disincentives for turning up, so much so that it is difficult to make much headway on the basis of turnout alone.

A different measure, discussed by Bernhard Wessels, seems to point to what might be termed 'reasonable satisfaction' with the operation of elections (Wessels 2011). These data suggest that the key variable determining whether or not we feel that elections help us to be represented is whether there is a meaningful distinction between the options available. Where there is a span of candidates or parties demonstrating real difference in terms of policies, we feel better represented. Where those differences are regarded as minor or trivial, so our satisfaction diminishes. As we shall see, 'real choice' is a concept under stress given the nature of contemporary governance. As sovereignty becomes more complex, so there is often a diminishing sense that incoming governments are able to exercise real choices in connection with key policies, particularly in the economic sphere.

Membership of political parties

If a sense of real choice is important in generating levels of satisfaction with the electoral process, then key to a healthy representative system is that there be political parties able to articulate different policies, different values and a different vision of how a given society or community might govern itself. This is particularly the case in parliamentary systems, but also in presidential systems where party political affiliations are well entrenched. Here the news seems to be much worse as far as gauging the health of representative politics is concerned. The membership of the major political parties across much of the developed world is in freefall (Mair and Van Biezen 2001; Hay 2007; Anon 2010; Whiteley 2011). This is particularly the case in Europe, which has seen membership of parties as a proportion of the electorate fall from around 25 to 30% of the electorate to less than 2 to 3% in many cases. Interestingly, the phenomenon is the same in countries like Australia where voting is compulsory and thus where there is no question of 'opting out' or turning one's back on the electoral process. The two main parties in Australia, the Liberals and Labour, have between 40,000 and 50,000 members each, representing around 1% of the electorate. By way of contrast, GetUp!, an online advocacy network, counts 700,000 supporters, and Collingwood, an Australian Rules Football Club, has 77,000 members (Granger 2013).

This steep decline in membership has several ramifications for considering the matter of representation. Firstly, it means that political parties can find themselves short of resources as they leak members. As large organizations with offices to maintain and campaigns to fund, they need to seek out other sources of support, not least from big business, banks and corporations. In response to this development there is currently a lively debate about the need or desirability for the public funding of political parties (Van Biezen 2004). The stakes are high. In the context of declining membership, should we leave political parties to snuggle up to corporations and other private bodies who naturally expect their interests to be well represented in the parties' programmes? Or do we regard the existence of political parties as a 'public good' and thereby deserving of financial support from the state? It is significant that entities purporting to advance the needs and interests of ordinary people have had to put the begging bowl out to secure funding to keep themselves going. How have we come to such a sorry state of affairs?

The dominant interpretation of this development is that political parties are failing to connect with the public (Dalton 2002: Pt III; Norris 2002; Van Biezen 2004). Parties are locked in a vicious circle: the fewer citizens who sign up, the closer they need to get to sources of financial support like business; the closer they get to business, the less attractive they look to the ordinary citizen, and so on. Yet assuming all this to be true, a further puzzle is posed. If it was the case that the reason for the decline of political parties is that they are getting too close to private interests, then one might expect to see a flourishing of political parties that *challenge* private interests, and that take it upon themselves to contest dominant or mainstream politics, however defined. Yet even parties of the left and far left, parties whose rationale is to challenge the *status quo*, have singularly failed to capitalize on what seems otherwise to be a moment of political opportunity. They have taken *votes* in advanced democracies – as, for example, in France, where far left parties have polled up to 15% in recent presidential elections. But they have not translated this into *membership*, or, what equates to the same thing, real grassroots support. The one category of party that does seem to be doing well is 'anti-political' parties, such as the Tea Party in the US, UKIP in the UK, Beppe Grillo's 5SM in Italy, Golden Dawn in Greece and the Pirates across Europe and elsewhere. Yet the attraction of such parties is that they promise to be 'different'. They style themselves as outside of the mainstream, 'parties for the rest of us', 'parties without politicians', or movements *as opposed to* parties.

Why does the decline of political parties matter? It's certainly part of the self-image of parliamentary systems that political parties are a vital point of mediation between ordinary citizens and the government or executive. An account of democracy that sees citizen involvement as involving turning out to vote once every four or five years surely offers a pretty impoverished vision. Since the advent of political parties in the nineteenth century and the contest for power via elections, political commentary has often stressed that parties play a vital role in enlivening democracy, in permitting ordinary citizens to be involved in a way that takes us beyond the mere marking of a ballot paper with an 'X' (Dalton 2002). As political parties decline in terms of mass membership, it is only to be expected that the leaders of such parties become less influenced by the wishes of the grassroots membership as opposed to the major funders and other groups with power and resources that may be needed to keep the party going. So we are left with a small elite grouping that is more attuned to the views and opinion of funders, the media and interest groups than its own membership. Elections become 'presidential', focused almost exclusively on the particular qualities of the competing leaders. Politics as a contest of values and different visions more nearly resembles a battle between business executives for the vote of the board.

Going back to Wessels' analysis, it seems on these terms more likely that voters will become alienated from the political process as a contest between 'real choices' becomes one between identikit middle-class men and women for political favour. This is a long way from the classic defences of party-based democracy, which stress how representation can be a proxy for participation as long as the different views and interests at large in society are somehow reflected in the different party offerings (Duverger 1959; Sartori 2005). If elections become personalized, if they focus on leadership qualities as opposed to policies, then the sense of elections as moments when genuine choices and alternatives are presented to a community disappears into a televisual display of forced smiles and perfect teeth, albeit without the entertainment value of Eurovision or *The X Factor*.

Trust in politicians

A functioning system of governance requires that those who govern do so not just on the basis of a mandate from the electorate, but also on the basis of the firm belief that they will govern in the interests of the nation, of the people. Authority is predicated on trust, or else government requires force in order to function. With this in mind, the collapse of confidence in the integrity of the political class is extraordinary and deeply worrying (Dalton 2004: Ch. 2; Flinders 2012; Della Porta 2013). Recent research shows that politicians are amongst the least trusted groups in society, that we don't trust political parties and that governments themselves cannot be trusted (Kaldor et al. 2012). If we don't trust our representatives, then it is but a short step to querying how long the system can continue.

In Australia, for example, trust in the 'pollies' or political class has nosedived (Goot 2002; Markus 2013). Certainly there is a history behind this contempt which helps us to explain why politicians are held in such low regard. Corruption has been, if not endemic, then a regularly enough occurring feature of Australian political life for the general public to be guarded about seeing politicians in a better light. What is curious is that, as with Nordic countries, politicians in Australia are not distant, far-away figures. They are not unapproachable in the manner that might apply where the security risks are greater, and politicians live sheltered lives in fortified premises. Politicians generally live in the communities they represent, amongst

21

ordinary people. Julia Gillard, former Prime Minister of Australia, famously lived in a simple bungalow in a modest neighbourhood of Melbourne. Tony Abbott has similarly remained in his family home in Frenchs Forest, an unremarkable suburb in northern Sydney. Yet despite their ordinariness and approachability, neither has managed to tame the media or public opinion: 'Another bloody polly'.

The story is a familiar one across mature democracies (Dalton 2004). Is the collapse in trust warranted? Is it really the case that politicians are much less trustworthy than other maligned groups in society? Probably not. But this isn't the point. As Pierre Rosanvallon argues, politicians are being set up to fail by the very nature of the system of representation (Rosanvallon 2011: 177). On the one hand, they are partisan figures. They emerge out of the context of a political party or political grouping that has a particular vision of how to govern the community that differs from the vision or set of values of the other candidates and parties in the electoral process. During that electoral moment we see them as defenders of a particular vision, as opposed to representatives of what Rosanvallon calls 'the generality'. On being elected, they then have to shed that partisan image and take on the mantle of a monarchic or presidential figure who governs in the interest of the *whole*, as opposed to part of it. What seems to be the case is that the public is less accepting of this process of transformation than it used to be. Paradoxically, the attempt by politicians to cast themselves as ordinary men or women, as 'people like us', works too well. 'Proximity' dispels the aura of mystery that formally underpinned their authority. It's their very ordinariness that poses a problem in creating that image of monarchic authority needed to represent the generality. So we don't trust them. We see politicians in much the same way as we see others who seek to present themselves as impartial or disinterested yet who have a fiduciary or financial interest in a particular outcome: two-faced. What, we might ask, is the common denominator between lawyers, estate agents and second-hand car salesmen? They are all professions where there is an almost tangible tension between the claim to represent the needs and interests of the client versus the needs and interest of the firm in making a profit. Much the same can be said of the role of the politician. All too often the rhetoric of acting in 'the name of the people' hides a partisan commitment to acting in the name of a very particular set of interests.

The net result of the erosion of trust is that the figure of the politician is now regarded as a figure of contempt. One will now strain to hear anyone in office describe themselves as a politician. The leaders of populist parties, and the anti-political parties mentioned above, make great play of their distance from the figure of the politician. It is a classic populist ploy, whether of the left or the right, to cast oneself as an anti-establishment figure, a person from beyond or outside the political class, 'a soccer mum'. This feeds a particular repertoire or performance that seeks to show the ordinariness and down-to-earth nature of the anti-political politician (Moffitt and Tormey 2014). We don't trust politicians, we don't like them, and woe betide anyone who begins to look and sound like 'a politician'.

Interest in politics

Political scientists worry about our interest in and knowledge of mainstream politics, and they are right to do so. Boredom, indifference and apathy are the enemies of the representative bond. Democracies rely on the existence of an active meaningful democratic culture, and this means a culture of questioning and interrogating what it is the politicians do so that in turn they can give reasons for their policies and their stance on the great issues of the day. Without critical interrogation, politics is reduced to 'governance', the rubber stamping of policies and procedures that have been decided elsewhere, behind our backs, and beyond critical scrutiny. Without scrutiny we have executive rule, rule by technocrats, 'post-democracy', as Colin Crouch memorably puts it (Crouch 2004). What are the relevant measures?

One way of seeking to put flesh on the bones of the assumption is to look at the content of the media. As has been well documented, coverage of politics in the media has changed markedly over the past half-century (Street 2001; Meyer and Hinchman 2002; Corner and Pels 2003). In the 1960s a newspaper like *The Times* of London would have carried six or seven pages of commentary on Parliament and the work of the Cabinet. This would increase in times of crisis or during elections. It was for this reason that it was called 'a paper of record'. If one wanted a comprehensive picture of day-to-day politics, then there was no better way of getting a feel for what was going on than reviewing back copies of *The Times*. Today, coverage of Parliament is usually confined to a page or less, and some of that may well be in the form of a sketch whose main purpose is to poke fun at proceedings. The rest of the paper carries the mix that has now become standard in the Anglo-Saxon world: sport, lifestyle, 'snippet news', celebrities, diets. It's not quite 'tits, bums and QPR', which is how one famously cynical journalist described the content of his own newspaper, but it's not far off (Thomas 2004). Politics and politicians do not sell newspapers.

The broadcast media are hardly any better. Long gone from public broadcasting in many democracies are the 'talking head' programmes devoted to the serious discussion of politics. Where such commentary exists, it is now confined to 'the graveyard slot' late at night, at Sunday lunchtimes, or it is exiled to obscure or little-watched channels such as A-PAC in Australia. Programmes about politics or political topics have to be spiced up, televisual, dramatic. They have to be 'infotainment' rather than a way in which people gain understanding or knowledge of how politics works. The rise of the 'shock jock', a staple in the Anglo-Saxon context, is all too telling. It seems to be more gripping to listen to someone take an extreme line on the matters of the day, to rip into unsuspecting politicians, than to listen to a sober analysis of the budget or foreign affairs. One has to *go looking* for serious commentary as opposed to expecting it as part of the usual diet of programming on TV or on the radio. As the numbers of those looking decline, so coverage is relegated to the periphery of daily life.

In view of the above, it should hardly be surprising that the level of understanding or knowledge displayed by many citizens about their political systems, about the activities of ministers or politicians, is at a low ebb. This is not the same as saying that people are uninterested in politics or that they have little understanding of other facets of political life, which is often the conclusion reached. It is, rather, to say that the affairs of the political class, of mainstream politics, have become of little interest to many citizens. So much is evident to those who make a living teaching politics to university students. It's now no longer a contradiction to note that someone can be passionate about, for example, animal rights or climate change and yet have very little knowledge of the key features of his or her own political system (Bennett 1998). 'Politics' for the concerned individual has changed key; it has become a matter of issues, injustices, campaigns, less so of the regular operation and functioning of a political system.

So this is further grist to the mill for political commentary worried about the direction in which representative politics is heading. If citizens are ignorant of key facts about their own political system, then it seems they are more likely to turn to the extremes, to populism or to anti-politics. Ignorance from this point of view can be read as a form of alienation. We are alienated from politicians and the political system. We should not be surprised that electorates are therefore keen to 'punish politicians', to disparage the results of their efforts to make our lives better.

The picture looks bleak. The overwhelming image we are left with surveying the variables of interest to political commentary is decay. As recently as the 1960s, representative politics seemed healthy and vibrant. Electorates turned out in their millions, enthusiastically joined political parties, trusted politicians and the apparatus of governance to act in the best interests of the community, and showed considerable knowledge and interest in the political mainstream. Now we are reluctant voters, and it seems becoming more reluctant as we are asked to vote more frequently and engage with the different scales at which politics takes place. The vast majority of citizens in the advanced democracies have little to do with political parties, leaving the latter to a dwindling number of diehards, political geeks and professional power-seekers. The term 'politician' has become a byword for sleaze, incompetence and self-serving. Citizens in advanced democracies care little for the affairs of the political class, except when 'affair' can be read as a bit of salacious gossip.

Given this, it is unsurprising that the mood amongst expert commentators is bleak. It's an intuitive response. A political logic that seemed to work so well at one level is apparently faced with obsolescence. On the other hand we are still left with the puzzle of the 'reinvention of politics', the emergence of new 'subterranean' politics, and how this connects to the decline of representative politics of the kind we have been discussing. So far we've heard a lot about what's lacking – voters, party members and an interested and engaged electorate. What about those who are *fully committed* to politics, to making things better, to mobilizing people, to organizing communal life? What about the rising tide of activists, concerned citizens, the politically literate, involved in politics beyond or outside the mainstream? What do we learn about representative politics studying their initiatives, practices, self-descriptions?

Contours of a crisis II: the view from the margin

At this point it will be useful to switch tack and consider the crisis from outside mainstream electoral politics of the kind we have been discussing. Politics is more than just elections. It's also about people getting organized, mobilized, to contest power from outside as well as inside the framework of elections. For the past couple of centuries much of this work has been undertaken by political parties, in particular the many socialist and communist parties that were established towards the end of the nineteenth century and in the early twentieth century to defend, and indeed represent, the interests of ordinary men and women.

Today, however, the stakes are rather different, given the collapsing confidence in the practices of political representation, which in turn leaves a gap for other forms and styles of politics to resonate, to be picked up and become part of the overall picture of crisis we are seeking to describe. Three of the more discussed cases amongst those taking an interest in non-mainstream, non-electoral politics include: (1) the emergence of the *Zapatistas and 'Zapatismo'*; (2) the *World Social Forum*, a wonderfully messy experiment in non-representative politics; and (3) *Occupy Wall Street*, which seeks to stir the 99% without as it were leading it. A brief glance at each will offer further clues as to what is going on.

The Zapatistas

The Zapatistas, or *Ejército Zapatista de Liberación Nacional* (EZLN), is a much commented upon and written about insurgent 'rebel army' that at first glance seems familiar from the history of Latin American revolutionary movements. Composed initially of a mix of indigenous malcontents, students and would-be revolutionary leaders, the Zapatistas came to public attention on a propitious date: 1 January 1994. This was the day when the North American Free Trade Agreement, or NAFTA, between Mexico, Canada and the US came into effect. The agreement promised open borders between the three countries, and the opportunity to exploit Mexico's considerable natural resources by North American corporations. This posed a threat to the way of life of indigenous groups in the southern part of Mexico who live off the land and rely on access to forests and wildlife in order to keep themselves alive. The Zapatistas joined forces with villagers in the Chiapas region to fend off Mexican federal forces as well as paramilitary groups hired by landowners to protect their private interests. The goal initially was to force the government to reconsider its position and to guarantee local indigenous groups access to land notwithstanding NAFTA. However, with the government showing little sign of wishing to negotiate, the forty or so communes declared themselves 'an autonomous zone' beyond and outside the jurisdiction of the federal state. Notwithstanding the regular incursions by the army and paramilitaries, the zone remains intact after two decades, sustained in large measure by the efforts of numerous solidarity groups, supporters and well-wishers who cottoned on to the Zapatistas as emblematic of a new phase of militancy in the face of 'neoliberalism'.

26

The relevance of the Zapatistas for our topic relates most immediately to the position of Subcomandante Insurgente Marcos (Rafael Guillen Vicente). Until he stepped down in May 2014, Marcos was one amongst several spokespeople for the 'Zapatista movement', but easily the most recognizable. He has become a Che Guevara-like figure for elements of the left, his pensive expression, balaclava and pipe as familiar as Che's beret and heroic countenance. This is due to the reception of Marcos's speeches and writings, which have been translated into many different languages and which resulted in him becoming the face of the Zapatistas' 'postmodern rebellion' (Burbach 2001). So what has he done or said that is so different?

Firstly, as Marcos himself relates the matter, he was drawn to radical politics on terms that will be familiar to anyone who has studied twentieth-century politics. He was young, disillusioned with capitalism and with Mexico's corrupt and creaking political system. He wanted to improve the condition of the poor and in particular of indigenous groups, which suffer more than most owing to their remoteness and lack of access to power and influence. He wanted to bring leadership to the otherwise ramshackle rebels who were prepared to rally to their cause. According to his own account, encountering the indigenous themselves led him to a change of heart and a change of approach. It occurred to him that the indigenous peasants already knew what they wanted. This was to exercise some control over their lives, to have access to lands, and to live decent lives where others respected their customs and way of life. Little else mattered. From this simple observation Marcos drew the conclusion that the role he had imagined for himself, that is, as a revolutionary intellectual able to show the peasants the path to a better, more emancipated existence, was redundant. The choice was either to ignore peasant wishes and to impose upon them an external perspective based on revolutionary ideology, or to help them realize their own aims and ambitions in a manner that suited the peasants, not him. He chose the latter. In doing so he renounced the legacy of revolutionary politics, the role of the intellectual as representative of the objective needs and interests of the represented, the peasants of the Chiapas region. He chose instead to make himself subject to the opinions and instructions of the peasants themselves.

From this simple gesture Marcos and the Zapatistas evolved a relationship with the peasant communes that appears to reverse the traditional relationship between the vanguard party or movement and the peoples they are supposed to represent. Several phrases were spun to describe this relationship which have gone on to become part of

27

the legacy of 'alter-politics' around the world. They include the idea of *Mandar Obedeciendo* ('Govern Obeying'). This is the idea that those 'in charge' or 'leading' exercise power on the basis that they directly obey the wishes of those who are themselves subject to it. No one exercises authority or power because of their position or because 'they know best'. Each of the villages within the autonomous zone holds regular meetings to gauge the feelings of the inhabitants and to feed back decisions to the Zapatistas. There are numerous other phrases and watchwords that have become part of the Zapatista lexicon: *Antipoder Contra Poder* ('Anti-power against Power'); *Todo Para Todos, Nada Para Nosotros* ('Everything for Everyone, Nothing for Ourselves'); *Queremos un Mondo Donde Quepan Muchos Mundos* ('We want a World Where Many Worlds Fit'). Each slogan (and there are many more) underlines their rejection of a leadership function in favour of a stance of solidarity and common cause with those struggling to maintain dignity and respect.[1]

Marcos himself sought to play down his centrality to the movement using a variety of devices to avoid the perception that he represented or embodied the movement. He used several *noms de plumes* (e.g. 'Delegate Zero', 'Don Durito') to de-emphasize the role of 'Marcos', and to show a different face depending on the context he was operating under and the message he wanted to convey. On occasion he disappeared from view or adopted a posture of silence in order to take the focus away from himself and to allow others room to speak and to be listened to. Thus after a more or less constant stream of declarations and writings in the early 2000s, Marcos made no public utterances for eighteen months. When he did eventually return to the fray it was to offer a rebuke to those hostile to the approach taken by the Zapatistas in relation to the leadership or representative function, which of course they had repudiated. The pamphlet was entitled *I Shit on All the Revolutionary Vanguards of This Planet*, which requires no further comment (Marcos 2003).

Why should we read any significance in the actions of a small number of rebels tucked away in the Lacondon Forest in a corner of Mexico – a kind of contemporary approximation of Asterix and the Gauls in their fight against the imperious Romans? Isn't this all marginal to the lives and interests of ordinary people?

At one level it is. The Zapatistas are a small and fairly insignificant force even in the context of the national politics of Mexico, let alone politics in other parts of the world. On the other hand, the Zapatistas are often criticized for being *overly* influential, and Marcos was regularly accused of hogging the activist limelight (McKinley 2005). What appears to be the case, nonetheless, is that the Zapatistas' message and example have resonated in a way that few struggles at the margin have matched in the past two decades. They have connected with other movements of the poor, particularly across Latin America, such as the *Movimento de Sem Terra*, or landless movements, with the *Via Campesina*, with the movements of indigenous peoples in Bolivia and Equador. Zapatista slogans have appeared in protests across the rest of the world, and, as we shall see, in the pronouncements of political parties such as the Catalonian Independence Party (CUP) seeking to reconstitute themselves as parties of the 'street'. They have inspired solidarity movements and initiatives such as the WOMBLES (White Overalls Movement Building Libertarian Effective Struggles) and *Ya Basta*. They have been taken up as exemplars of 'anti-power' by writers such as John Holloway, author of *Change the World Without Taking Power* (2002), and rock bands such as Rage Against the Machine, in turn entering popular culture. More generally, they have been seen as exemplars for a different kind of political practice, one that seeks to put power at the service of communities, rather than to make communities subject to the deliberations of far-away representatives (Katzenberger 1995; Holloway and Pelaez 1998; Tormey 2006).

None of this is to claim that the Zapatista model of 'good governance' has some sort of normative validity or that it offers a blueprint for complex modern societies. Nor should we imagine that there aren't problems in terms of its implementation. There are. What we are interested in here is the nature of the crisis facing representative politics. What the Zapatista case illuminates is an emergent discourse that sees representative politics and the function of representing others as *complicit in injustice* – not, as many radicals previously held, the basis for struggling against injustice. The injustice in this case is the continued marginalization of indigenous peoples, who are then forced to mobilize by the terms of a free trade agreement that worsens the condition of the very poor living in far-flung corners of the country. The association between electoral politics and a colonial and marginalizing form of politics is a persistent theme in development studies and critical global studies (Duffield 2007; Mignolo 2012). But it's also the injustice of silencing and marginalization produced by what is termed 'vanguardism', or the insistence that intellectuals take the lead in telling the very poor, or marginalized, what kind of political strategy they should be adopting. 'Anti-power' is in this sense not just a warding off of the state and its mechanisms for managing 'pluralism'. It's also a stance in relation to knowledge, truth and power – who wields it, and in whose name.

The World Social Forum (WSF)

Soon after the Zapatista insurrection in 1994 a wave of 'anticapitalist' or anti-globalization protests broke out, signalling to many commentators the end of a period of liberal triumphalism and the beginning of a new wave of contestation (e.g. Tormey 2004). The 'Battle of Seattle' of November 1999 remains the most iconic of the large-scale Summit protests. The idea for a World Social Forum emerged in a dialogue between the editors of *Le Monde Diplomatique* and the Brazilian Workers Party (PT), whose leader, 'Lula' de Silva, had recently been elected President of the country. The idea was to create a space for dialogue and discussion which could provide the basis for proposing positive initiatives as well as reflecting on the injustices of the global system (Fisher and Ponniah 2003; Mertes and Bello 2004; Sen 2004). This would be in contrast to the invitation-only World Economic Forum, which offers corporate leaders, politicians and analysts a stage to mull over global affairs in the luxury surroundings of the hotel complex in Davos, Switzerland.

The first forum was held in Porto Alegre, Brazil, in 2001. Twelve thousand activists attended, exceeding the more optimistic predictions as to how many would show up. This led to the demand that the WSF become an annual event. The Forum idea quickly caught on in other ways, inspiring the creation of continental, regional, national and subnational social forums. There were also forums for particular groups such as indigenous people and particular topics such as the environment and the place of women's struggle in society. Subsequent meetings of the WSF attracted many more participants – over 100,000, according to some estimates. It is little exaggeration to describe the WSF as the single most important initiative associated with the emergence of 'global civil society'.

Of interest for our purposes is the rhetoric and language used to describe the initiative. The original Charter of the WSF notes that it 'brings together and interlinks . . . organizations and movements of civil society from all the countries in the world', but does not intend 'to be a body representing world civil society'. Article 6 goes on to state:

> The meetings of the World Social Forum do not deliberate on behalf of the World Social Forum as a body. No one, therefore, will be authorized, on behalf of any of the editions of the Forum, to express positions claiming to be those of all its participants. The participants in the Forum shall not be called on to take decisions as a body, whether by vote or acclamation, on declarations or proposals for action that would

commit all, or the majority, of them and that propose to be taken as establishing positions of the Forum as a body. It thus does not constitute a locus of power to be disputed by the participants in its meetings, nor does it intend to constitute the only option for interrelation and action by the organizations and movements that participate in it.

Article 9 goes on to state that

the World Social Forum will always be a forum open to pluralism and to the diversity of activities and ways of engaging of the organizations and movements that decide to participate in it, as well as the diversity of genders, ethnicities, cultures, generations and physical capacities, providing they abide by this Charter of Principles. Neither party representatives nor military organizations shall participate in the Forum.

What do we learn from the Charter? Overwhelmingly, that the WSF is both a *non*-representative and an *anti*-representative initiative. It doesn't speak for anyone, and no one can speak for it. 'It' doesn't have the character of a political actor that can represent or be represented. Those who seek to attend as representatives of parties are not welcome either, even if they are members of the Brazilian PT, which helped create it. Nor does the WSF welcome other kinds of representatives, including those from 'military organizations'. Ironically this has meant that the Zapatistas, the poster movement for many '*alter-mondialistas*', have been prevented from attending the official Forum meetings. They have instead been forced to hold *encuentros* (encounters) and events outside and beyond the official gathering.

Reading between the lines, what becomes clear is that the founders of the Forum wanted to make a clean break with the legacy of representative politics. They wanted the Forum to be a different kind of body to a political party or a social movement. They wanted it to be 'open' and 'pluralist', as opposed, one surmises, to the 'closed' and 'monist' – or ideological and programmatic – form of political parties. They could see that labelling an initiative a party or a movement would include some, but exclude many more. It also implied hierarchy, bureaucracy, offices, leadership and all the other trappings associated with conventional political organizations. They wanted to avoid such a fate. They weren't seeking followers, members or those looking for answers or ready-made solutions. They wanted to create a new kind of body, a dialogical 'space' of a contingent, provisional kind that would facilitate experimentation and creativity.

We can put to one side the question of whether the founders have achieved what they set out to create, and there are many, including enthusiastic supporters, who argue that they didn't (Sen 2004).

31

What we are interested in is the image of representative politics being painted. It's an undeniably negative one that says that representative politics, the politics of political parties and mainstream organizations, is a politics of closed minds, of monologues, of subservience to a dominant narrative or ideology. Needless to say, this was picked up by Marxist critics of the initiative, who were, understandably, as sceptical about the effectiveness of the Forum as the Charter was dismissive of political parties. Isn't it just a talking shop? Doesn't it dilute or disperse the energies of activists? How can one imagine changing the world on the basis of an experimental space? One group of prominent Marxists led by the noted theorist Samir Amin wrote up their concerns in what became known as 'The Bamako Appeal' to coincide with the 'Polycentric' WSF held in 2006 (Sen 2007). They urged that the Forum be transformed into a political movement capable of contesting power, a New International that would assemble the poor and exploited of the world behind capable leaders committed to overthrowing neoliberalism. The appeal arrived in a flurry, caused a stir and quickly faded, along with it the hope of a new mega-party able to represent the global poor in the battle against the world's elites.

More telling perhaps was the criticism that the WSF was not consistent or rigorous enough in its rejection of representative politics (Sen 2004). Critics have pointed out that, for example, the composition and deliberations of the International Committee that superintend the WSF are too opaque, and – interestingly – the Committee is not representative enough of those who attend the Forum. Others complain about the WSF forums giving star billing to certain well-known figures (Noam Chomsky, Naomi Klein, Susan George, etc.), undermining the ambition to promote a *dialogue* as opposed to a sequence of monologues. There have been critics of the middle-class character of the WSF, and the fact that it is run by organizations from the global North, including many religious bodies such as Caritas. It's little surprise to find therefore that many forums have been occasions for the holding of parallel 'counter-forums' or 'alter'-forums beyond the main event, permitting a yet more emphatically anti-representative, participatory style of interaction to take place.

Occupy Wall Street (OWS)

The GFC marked by the collapse of Lehman Brothers in 2008 gave fresh impetus to those seeking to contest the power of the elites, now sounding somewhat less triumphalist in the wake of a collapsing economic paradigm: 'financialized' capitalism. Inspired by the new mood of militancy demonstrated across the world and in particular the Middle East, activists and many others touched by hardship went on the offensive. In November 2011 a sit-down protest in the symbolic place of financial power, Wall Street, quickly snowballed into an occupation of nearby Zucotti Park. Protests and demonstrations are by their nature fleeting, transitory events. They come and they go. An occupation, on the other hand, is a powerful gesture. It is a permanent (or quasi-permanent) reminder of the anger and frustration of many ordinary people at the actions of elites who seemed only too keen to help the banks, less so those who lost their jobs or livelihoods as a result of the GFC.

Occupy Wall Street resonated across the US. It is estimated that 1.5 million citizens in 600 cities and towns across every state took part in an occupation, usually in a prominent public space (Castells 2012: 163). Such was the force of the gesture that it took off around the world. Indeed there were few countries that didn't have an occupation somewhere at some time. There were other kinds of occupation as well: virtual occupations, occupations of particular events and particular professions. In my own discipline, there is an 'Occupy IR Theory' group. But what the media and wider public wanted to know was what was Occupy for? What did Occupy want? The questions seemed reasonable enough, and yet answers were difficult to come by. To whom should one be speaking to get an answer? Who was in charge? How could one get hold of the demands or the analysis of those participating?

What quickly became apparent is that participants in the occupations came to the view that the gesture of occupying public space was at one level enough. It symbolized collective anger and frustration without committing participants to any particular political programme, analysis or manifesto. Occupation itself posed questions (*Why are they sitting there? What are they angry about?*) without presupposing that there was one answer or one solution. The point was to keep the occupation intact, which in turn meant developing organizational skills that permitted an instant community to manage its own affairs whilst remaining true to the anti-elitism identified by the key slogan of Occupy, 'We are the 99%.' Collective energies were directed at managing assemblies, creating groups concerned with particular problems or particular issues confronting the occupation, communicating with other Occupy groups and indeed with other organizations and movements. The suggestion aired by prominent figures such as Slavoj Žižek and Alex Callinicos that in order to confront elites Occupy had to develop a programme and a strategy for contesting power fell on unsympathetic ears (Žižek 2012a). Why was this?

It seems clear from the various accounts of those involved with Occupy that participants were resistant to embarking on the first steps down the road of a movement or political party with clearly articulated goals and ambitions (Wark 2011; Castells 2012). As with the WSF, there seemed to be a desire, widely felt, to be as inclusive as possible. This meant not doing or saying anything that would create a distinction or a point of contention that would drive some away at the same time as it might encourage others to join. It seemed that the trope of 'the 99%' could only be promoted or safeguarded if Occupy permitted multiple readings by those who encountered it. One OWS banner summed up the matter. It read: 'Slogan Pending'. This neatly encapsulates the idea at the heart of the initiative that discussion, dialogue, deliberation, presuppose not *knowing* what happens next, but rather deciding what happens next *together*. The task of slogan or strategy creation could only be envisaged as a collective one, something that engaged everyone who identified with the initiative.

So Occupy seemed to embrace a style of politics that made a break with or queried representative politics considered in two ways. It queried dominant or mainstream politics. In distinguishing between the 99% and the 1%, it undermined the claim that political elites represent us, The People. It said that the 99% are not represented; that the 1% represent themselves, enrich themselves, promote themselves at the cost of the 99%. Yet equally, by putting on hold the question of what to do next, Occupy implicitly resisted the logic associated with traditional political movements and parties which have sought to represent the needs and interests of the 99%. The absence of a manifesto or programme, regarded as a 'lack' by the media and by elements of the left seeking to develop the gesture, could also be read as an anti-vanguardist statement and by extension an invitation for anyone who felt some affinity with Occupy to become involved (Tormey 2012).

Marxists and many others query the effectiveness of such a politics, particularly when Occupy, whilst astonishingly popular at one level, was still an initiative considered in global terms to engage only a small fraction of the relevant populations. Occupy sought to engage 'the 99%', but of course a large portion of the empirically existing 99% either didn't engage with it or would have disagreed with it. Yet this doesn't detract from the meaning of Occupy or what it symbolized as far as representative politics is concerned. Whether Marxists wish to acknowledge it or not, Occupy resonated with huge numbers of people, particularly young people, in a way that traditional political movements or parties have been unable to match in the last few decades. It succeeded in generating an enormous amount of commentary on the relationship between capitalism, power and democracy. It also offered a little glimpse of a style of activism, often called 'prefigurative', that seeks less to develop programmes and blueprints than to show directly the possibility of living in accordance with different values, a different ethos and a directly democratic mode of organizing communal life. In doing so it connects back to a different style or tradition of politics, finding its roots in the various experiments in communal living associated with earlier movements such as the Levellers, with decolonizing movements such as Gandhi's *Satayagraha* movement, with Havel's Velvet Revolution, with the 'people power' movements that accompanied the fall of the Berlin Wall, and with the struggles against neo-colonialism, nepotism and cronyism in countries such as Myanmar and the Philippines, and of course in the Chiapas.

Conclusion

Narrating the crisis of representative politics is part science and part art. Political scientists stand on the former site of the equation. They largely agree that the variables show a worrying trend as far as representative politics is concerned. On their key variables, it is difficult to avoid the conclusion that the legitimacy and credibility of mainstream politics are in question, saved perhaps by a collective sense that democracy remains 'the least worst form of government'. Those of us interested in a wider definition of politics as including the activities of social movements, protest groups, activists of all shapes and sizes, are faced with a picture that is more complex to capture in quantitative terms. We need to pay attention to what it is that activists say and do. We need to look at their pronouncements, declarations, charters. We need to read between the lines, and adopt styles of ethnographic, even hermeneutic, understanding. It's an art, and art does not lend itself to neat, summative conclusions, only suggestions for how developments might be read.

What can be inferred from contemporary developments is that the crisis of representation also infects unofficial, street, subterranean politics *as well as* mainstream, official politics, the politics of 'the politicians'. Something is altering in the contours of the political landscape. Representative politics is failing to engage. Other styles of politics are nudging towards, or suggestive of, some other way of thinking and doing politics. These attempts lack a systematic character, and some of them, as in the case of the WSF, are riddled with flaws of institutional design as well as operation. Nonetheless, non- or anti-representative politics has clearly resonated strongly, as these initiatives in their own way demonstrate. They have caught the imagination, particularly of young people. It's an excitement generated by a sense of a new departure, and a break with the 'old way of doing things'. At the same time it is much harder to see where such developments are going or what their lessons might be in more general terms. Are these just little eruptions to the order of things, a passing phase, idiosyncratic moments? Or are they harbingers of something else, some attempt to query, challenge and perhaps get *beyond* representation?

— 2 —

LOCATING 'REPRESENTATIVE POLITICS'

As we noted in the last chapter, the sense of representative politics being in crisis is pervasive. It infects not only mainstream politics, the politics of elections, political parties and politicians, but also street politics, the politics of political movements and those contesting the mainstream. The perception that representation and representative politics are flawed, dysfunctional or otherwise to be resisted, countered, avoided, seems to be becoming more widely shared. It's for this reason that I suggested in the introduction that we try to think about what is implied in representation and representing others as opposed to just examining particular instances of the failure of representative politics to engage discrete parts of the population or particular countries or particular kinds of political practice.

It's time to pose the question of the extent to which there is something in the idea of representation that is at the heart of the matter. In doing so, we will be running against the tide. Representation and representative politics are so intrinsic to a lot of thinking about how politics works, and indeed how it must work, that merely to pose the question of the 'future' of representative politics with the sense of wondering whether there is life after it is to set oneself at odds with much of the received wisdom on the matter. Fair enough, one might think. Representation is at one level utterly intrinsic to human existence. Language, for example, is a system of representation. Words stand in for, 'signify' or represent objects. We simply can't communicate with each other except via a system of representation. Theorists talk about the 'representative function of art', with the implication that art represents something outside or beyond itself. It stands in for something, evokes something, represents something – or not, in which case it is 'post-representative', which is to say, challenging or

37

questioning of representation. Getting closer to the subject of our discussion, representing others is something many of us do when attending meetings in the workplace, in a local club or association, or a school or college. Representing as 'standing in for' is often uncontentious. Indeed it's often a necessary and desirable means for avoiding the alternative: the requirement to spend half of one's life in meetings.

Representing others is a commonplace practice for citizens in modern settings. Yet perhaps it is the very banality of representation that gets in the way of interrogating representative politics as a mode or way of doing politics. Because it is so natural, everyday or normal, the temptation is to assume that it cannot be representation *itself* that is complicit in the travails of representative systems and representative politics. It must be some or other iteration of representation, some failed approach to institutional design that is at issue. Perhaps; but we won't know until and unless we set representative politics in some sort of context so that we can see where it came from, how it developed and where it is heading. It will therefore be useful to treat 'representative politics' *as if it was* a paradigm in Thomas Kuhn's sense, that is, as a stock of presuppositions and practices located in a specific historical and cultural context. The implication is that with changes in that context, so the assumptions underpinning the practice might themselves change in turn, undermining the 'naturalness' of the specific practice in question.

So in this chapter we seek to 'locate' representative politics, to give it a historical and contextual setting that will in turn help to establish what it means and how it has operated. Where did representative politics come from? What did it replace? Where is it going?

The origins of 'representation'

Notwithstanding the difficult-to-shift impression that representative politics has always been with us, in terms of the discourse on representation, how it works and what is involved, historians of ideas tend to agree that representation emerges within the occidental world as a specific problematic with the passage from feudalism to modernity (Manin 1997; Keane 2009). Indeed a number of commentators are even more specific, seeing Thomas Hobbes's *Leviathan*, published in 1651, as the first major work in English to deploy the language of representation to justify a particular political arrangement (e.g. Pitkin 1972; Brito Vieira and Runciman 2008). So why did representation appear as a specific problematic at this juncture? What prompted the need to be thinking about the legitimacy of governance by reference to how those who rule represent those who are subject to rule?

In order to get to grips with this issue we need to be thinking initially about what the transition from feudalism to modernity means and how this impacts the nature of political authority. Modernity is in social theory equated with a number of key developments:

- the emergence of nation states in Europe;
- the waning authority of the established Church, of orthodoxy;
- the emergence of new classes, groups, social movements, in the wake of industrialization, colonialism and urbanization.

The emergence of the nation state

Modernity is associated in terms of the evolution of political structures with the emergence of the nation state out of the variety of different political forms characterizing the feudal order (Poggi 1978; Bayly 2004; Pierson 2011). The latter included city states such as Florence and Genoa, principalities, fiefdoms and all manner of provisional political forms often the product of historical accident, personal ambition and avarice. Whilst countries were well established by this time, the degree of power able to be exercised by the state was limited by comparison to later centuries. Communication was slow, infrastructure lacking and travel laborious. It took days and weeks to get word from one end of a country to another. Monarchs were often dependent on maintaining a network of dependent nobles, who in turn had a strong sense of ownership and entitlement over their own lands. This was the source of considerable friction in countries such as England and France that sought to develop a sense of nationhood in the early modern period. Nevertheless, competition between states led to an intensification of efforts to control territory from the centre, not least to guarantee a flow of resources and men needed to fight the frequent wars with which the emerging colonial powers were involved (Sassen 2006). The transformation of territory in turn necessitated the transformation of political identities from those supporting and sustaining the feudal order to those sustaining the nation state. Loyalty to the person of the crown, to nobles, barons and princes gave way to the need for an 'imagined community' of the nation (Anderson 2006). Modernization was thus accompanied by a systematic process of nation-building to produce identities supportive of the transition. The idea of the 'self-determination of peoples' became intrinsic to the modern imagination and the basis

39

for thinking about legitimate political authority, notwithstanding the fact that it was rarely the People themselves who created the Nation, but the Nation – or state – that created a People who could then be represented.

The waning of religious orthodoxy

Modernity is also associated with important cultural movements that collectively serve to undermine a key source of political obligation in the feudal period: loyalty to the Church. The Renaissance brought forward the idea of universal humanism, or the idea that humanity was the author of its own destiny, not God. It's also associated with the works of those such as Niccolò Machiavelli who saw politics less as divinely inspired activity than as a contest of power necessitating pragmatic and even unethical behaviour to succeed. The Reformation unleashed a variety of heresies the impact of which was to query the basis of legitimacy in the mediaeval period: the unity of Church and state. Protestantism led to a proliferation of new political demands and movements seeking greater tolerance for non-orthodox religious belief and practices, for right to private conscience and for a separation of Church and state. The Enlightenment further undermined the hold of the religious imagination through extolling the application of the methods of the natural sciences to the study of all areas of human activity, including politics. It also brought forward the idea of political rights, of social and political improvement and of the centrality of freedom and autonomy as underpinning civilized society.

Mercantile capitalism and the first great transformation

Underpinned by colonial expansion, early modernity offered greater opportunities for self-enrichment through trade and commerce. This underpinned the development of industrialization in Europe, the taking over of once common land for 'improvement' or agri-industry and the creation of new industries to fuel further expansion. With such a remarkable transformation of economic fortunes, so social and political transformation followed in its wake. New classes emerged from the greater opportunities for trading. With wealth came the demand for greater power or 'representation' in the existing political structures, many of which reflected their origins in the feudal order. Industrialization and urbanization also led to the expansion of a new working class, which began gradually to supplant agricultural labour. Colonial expansion also meant an influx of subjects from colonized territories, leading to the transformation of the urban environment into a meeting ground for different ethnicities and identities. With the establishment of the printing press and the concomitant growth of literacy, a rapid dissemination of materials and information became possible. This all implied increased opportunity for messages and ideas to spread, further weakening the hold of the Church and feudal order on the imaginations of subject populations.

From absolutist to democratic representation

The net result of these changes is that a new basis of political legitimacy was required to fill the vacuum created by the waning of religious orthodoxy and doctrines such as the 'divine right of kings', by which monarchs and rulers had justified their hold on power. The language of representation served an important function in this respect, as Hobbes made clear in *Leviathan*. Representation implied a process of *re-presenting* the will of the collective. It thus promised a relationship of reciprocity and partnership between those who govern and those who are governed. This was famously expressed in the frontispiece of the original edition of *Leviathan*, which depicts a giant monarchical figure looming over his lands with sword in hand. On closer inspection the figure of the monarch is composed of hundreds of his own subjects collectively massed together to form 'the body politic'. The picture illustrates Hobbes's own account of representation, which stresses the origin of sovereign power in the will of the multitude, who collectively desire a singular authority to guarantee 'civil peace'. The implication is that it is the People who are the source of sovereign power, a proposition underpinned by the idea of a contract between the sovereign and the governed. Sovereigns did not have a right to rule, but were brought into being through the actions of the people.

Of note in terms of Hobbes's account is the fact that the form of representation he describes was *absolutist* not democratic. Hobbes believed that, to be effective, sovereigns needed to exercise absolute power and to have a unified character, whether in the form of a monarch or an assembly such as Parliament. Hobbes was therefore able to resolve the key dispute giving rise to the English Civil War. This was whether Parliament or King should be regarded as exercising legitimate sovereignty. Hobbes insisted that since the *form* the sovereign takes is irrelevant from the point of view of the *task* to be performed, securing peace, either could act as sovereign and by extension represent the people. Notwithstanding the fact that this distinction assumes great importance in later discussions of sovereignty, Brito Vieira and Runciman argue that 'we need to recognize that modern politics has always been, with respect to the central place of representation within it, a recognizably Hobbesian enterprise' (Brito Vieira and Runciman 2008: 60). Why?

As they and others explain, representation involves a *fiction*, albeit a necessary one as far as defenders of representative systems are concerned (Rosanvallon 2011: 13). The fiction is the idea that the people have brought the sovereign into being and that the latter is therefore nothing more than the will of the people brought to life. History suggests otherwise, as Hobbes knew well. Most states are historically the product of colonialism, conquest, partition, annexation, defeat or some other more or less violent process in which political authority is imposed on a given population. Hobbes understood that telling people that they should obey the sovereign because they have to is unlikely to be regarded by the latter as the basis for legitimate governance. Political authority requires some minimal 'consent' to work. Hobbes therefore asks us to imagine what life would be like if there were no political authority at all, but just a 'state of nature' or anarchy. The calculation Hobbes makes is that we are more concerned with our own *security* than we are with matters of deliberation or participation, and thus would consent if the question was ever posed as to whether we regard the sovereign as legitimate. So there is no violence in the idea of calling the sovereign a 'representative' on these terms. On the contrary, it offers us the *impression* of having an active role in shaping the behaviour of the sovereign. And in politics, as for so much else, impressions count.

The English Civil War offered evidence that, on the contrary, there are moments when the who and what of representation and political power assume great importance for ordinary people as well as political philosophers. Many of those fighting on the Parliamentary side did so on the basis that parliaments would be more accountable to the people than a hereditary monarch. Those who took part in the *Putney Debates* between various factions of Cromwell's army looked forward to the time when the needs and interests of ordinary people could be expressed through representatives who would be accountable to them in some fashion (Macpherson 1962; Hill 1972). Nor was it just the soldier yeomanry who worried about absolutist rule. It was also those emerging new classes of wealthy merchants and industrialists, intellectuals and philosophers. Theorists such as *John Locke* writing in the immediate decades after Hobbes were concerned about the prospect of absolutism, no matter how benign or benevolent it seemed to be. Whilst it was necessary for the state to represent the general interests of the people, it was also necessary to make sure that power did not congeal in the hands of a few, even less of one person. This would potentially endanger the newly won liberties and rights that accompanied the waning of absolutist and theological power.

From the late seventeenth century onwards, then, two concerns came to underpin the theory and practice of representative politics: *an ambivalence towards the state* and *an ambivalence towards the people – or demos.*

An ambivalence towards the state

Hobbes's account stressed that state power had to be absolute in order to guarantee peace. Later theorists were not so sure. We have already mentioned Locke, who, as a Protestant who had himself been victimized under Catholic rule, was unsurprisingly critical of Hobbes's absolutism. Locke articulated what became an important precept of liberalism when he argued that the right to life, liberty and property could not be transferred or given up to secure civil peace or security. They had to be regarded as the basis for civilized existence. Without rights, citizens are the playthings of rulers, prey to the whims and fancies of those who are accountable to no one but themselves. In thinking about the role of the state we therefore needed to start from the premise that state power be *limited* and that it should seek to promote the individual's natural rights above other considerations.

Much thought was given over the course of the eighteenth and nineteenth centuries as to how best to achieve this. Theorists such as *Montesquieu* in the early eighteenth century put forward ideas for a 'mixed constitution' separating the various functions of the state (executive, legislative, judicial) and dispersing them amongst different individuals and bodies. The doctrine of the 'separation of powers' was put forward as a way of constraining the power of the state and by extension the power of those who sought to use the state for their own purposes. Further elaboration followed from Alexander Hamilton and James Madison, key figures behind *The Federalist Papers* and the establishment of the American Constitution. If the separation of powers served to divide up the power of the central state, then federalism would do the same on the vertical axis, ensuring a degree of autonomy to the states that composed the union. 'States rights' became emblematic of the view that the central or federal state could not always be trusted to act in the best interests of the constituent parts of the union. The states themselves should be accorded the power to determine what was in their own best interests on certain key matters.

Accountability thus became an important element of thinking about the relationship between the state and the people. Hobbes's sovereign was, as noted, effectively unaccountable. This meant that the only way to get rid of the sovereign was through revolution. Representation has to imply a basis in a voluntary act to be meaningful. It moved from being an absolutist's charter towards being the basis for a relationship based on the idea of accountability. Citizens should be able to hold their representative or representatives to account. This in turn implied periodic election. It also meant that representatives should be thought of as having a *mandate* to govern, as opposed to a right or entitlement to govern. The implication was that citizens have the right to expect their representatives to act in accordance with the will of those represented.

Much discussion ensued about how this relationship should be configured (Pitkin 1972). Theorists such as *Edmund Burke* in the eighteenth century argued that representatives should be free to represent their constituency in whatever way they thought fit. The point of elections was to permit a contest between different representatives, not to mandate them to act directly on the wishes of constituents. This is what subsequently became the basis of the 'Trustee' model of political representation. We entrust a representative to look after our needs and interests but without binding him or her in terms of what that might imply in relation to any particular policy or proposal. Representatives, on this reading, are chosen on the basis of their personal qualities, integrity and judgement.

Others argued that representation meant some form of *delegation*, implying that it was the task of the representative to report accurately the feelings and opinions of those being represented. This understanding became the basis of the 'Principal–Agent' model of representation, which implies a relationship of a kind we otherwise associate with the hiring of a lawyer or stockbroker. The understanding is that the representative is under instruction to deliver certain outcomes based on the express preferences of the represented. Should the person who represents stray from those preferences too far, then the implication is that he or she should be 'recalled' or replaced with another person who better understands the preferences in question.

These distinctions rumble on today in discussions concerning what *exactly* is implied in the role of a democratically elected representative or politician, and there remains a lively debate concerning how best to capture the relationship between representatives and those represented (Mansbridge 2003; Rehfeld 2009; Disch 2011). The stakes are high, as we have already noted. Unrealistic expectations about what it is that our representatives could or might be doing are, according to many commentators, part of the reason why this relationship seems to have become so rocky (Norris 2011; Flinders 2012). Expecting representatives to behave like delegates, and not as individuals with their own views and opinions, means that we imagine that there should be some direct connection between how we cast our vote and the outcomes that are delivered thereby. On the other hand, if all we are doing is selecting individuals on the basis of their character or personality, then it should hardly be surprising that politics has come to resemble a beauty pageant rather than a process that results in a clear mandate to deliver certain outcomes.

An ambivalence towards the demos

Locke's fear of the state was primarily in response to the potential threat of the re-emergence of the absolutist monarchy in its ongoing contest with Parliament. As that threat receded, so the concern of liberal theorists moved from absolutism from above to absolutism from below. The revolutionary upheavals of 1789 and 1848 had shown how street protests could quickly take on a life of their own, becoming significant mobilizations that threatened to sweep away the existing order in favour of what came to be termed 'the tyranny of the majority'. The fear was that with the opening up of the political process through the introduction of elections, the *demos* might elect a government bent on ripping up those fundamental rights and freedoms in the quest for greater equality or 'social justice'.

Later liberal theorists were quite explicit about the need to avoid direct rule by the people. One of the greatest theorists of representative government, *J. S. Mill*, writing in the 1860s, made the point forcibly that the emergence of a form of democracy that permitted the *demos* to govern itself would likely lead to an intolerant majoritarian form of rule which would snuff out that individuality or eccentricity which he thought essential to social progress. Representation put in place a buffer between the *demos* and the state. This would make it difficult if not impossible for a government to be elected with a mandate radically to transform the social and economic basis upon which Mill thought liberty was based. As he put it, the purpose of representative government was 'not to permit people to govern themselves, but to prevent them from being misgoverned' (Mill 1972: 232).

By the middle of the nineteenth century, then, a key feature of representative government had been set, what later political scientists were unblushingly to term the 'rotation of elites'. How that rotation occurred was rather less important for many than what it implied: the prevention of tyranny from either above or below. The second term, 'elites', is itself a giveaway. Mill and other theorists of representation were just as determined to prevent rule by the people as they were the absolutism of monarchs or tyrants. Representation was regarded by many of its advocates as a mechanism for mediating political demands, preventing the emergence of radical agendas or anything else that might upset the *status quo*. Yet at the same time the introduction of elections changed the dynamic of representation in important ways. It implied above all else that those doing the representing were now accountable in some direct fashion to the populace. This is not to say that there were no further issues to worry those concerned about the quality of representation. There were many. Early elections in Europe and North America were often pretty roughshod affairs with all manner of corrupt practices such as 'gerrymandering', or the drawing up of electoral boundaries to favour a particular candidate, sitting alongside 'rotten boroughs' or the maintenance of tiny constituencies favouring a local patron or noble (Foot 2005). A glance at William Hogarth's 'Election' paintings of the eighteenth century is a wonderful counterpoint to the often manicured image of early democracy we sometimes get in the commentary: a world of booze, bribes and bawdiness that makes the hullabaloo over the behaviour of today's politicians look overblown.[1] However, the trajectory had been set: those exercising power had to be mindful of and accountable to those being represented. The people could not just be spoken for without reproach or return; they now had a direct stake in *who* spoke on their behalf. From being a largely passive element in politics, the people now had a stake in politics, albeit modestly framed and sometimes imperfectly executed. The long march had begun towards the establishment of representative democracy as the dominant form that democracy and indeed governance were to take over the course of the next two hundred years.

Representation and its critics

In a very brief discussion of this kind on the origins of representative politics it is easy to overlook the fact that the evolution of representative politics was highly contested. It was contested not only in terms of ideas about who or what should be represented, but also in terms of the idea that being represented could be considered the acme of political freedom. Arguably the most important critic of the emerging paradigm was *Jean-Jacques Rousseau*, a Geneva-born philosopher writing in the middle of the eighteenth century who became an iconic figure for the French Revolutionaries. Rousseau's view was that the practice of representative politics centred on the election of someone who would then exercise power on our behalf represented an abdication of our liberty. As he put it in 1762: 'The English people believes itself to be free; it is gravely mistaken; it is free only during the election of Members of Parliament; as soon as the Members are elected, the people is enslaved' (Rousseau 1985).

Rousseau was inspired by the Republican ideal of a self-governing community of equals with the active participation of each member in generating laws. Easier said than done, of course. Rousseau has often been cast as a proto-totalitarian who leans rather too heavily on the idea of shared virtue or a 'civic religion' to generate the sense of common purpose required in a self-governing community (Talmon 1961). Nevertheless, the idea that voting for representatives gives a thin basis to citizenship has been influential in terms of generating critiques of representative democracy. A number of the approaches mentioned in the introduction, such as the idea of strong democracy, republican democracy and indeed participatory democracy, were inspired directly or indirectly by Rousseau's thinking.

Similar criticisms, though with different recommendations as to how to address them, emerged in the critique of Enlightenment radicals such as *William Godwin*, a near contemporary of Rousseau. Godwin criticized the institution of the modern state on grounds that it divested society of the capacity to run its own affairs (Godwin 2013). The state was primarily an instrument of coercion guaranteeing the wealth and privilege of a few whilst everyone else toiled in their service. Representative institutions offered an image of self-governance which masked the reality of inequality and the perpetuation of privilege. Godwin looked forward to the time when 'reason' prevailed and humanity could see that inequality created conflicts which then necessitated the state. He regarded these conflicts as 'errors of judgement' that would be corrected through the application of sound reasoning. His work was foundational for the English radical tradition and later anarchists such as *Pierre-Joseph Proudhon* and *Peter Kropotkin*, who similarly argued that the function of the state was above all to protect property and the wealthy. It was therefore inequality that created the need for security and thus for the state. Eliminate the inequality generated by capitalism and the need for the state and political representation would disappear. Or so they hoped.

The most influential early critic of representative democracy, *Karl Marx*, agreed that the origins of the modern state lay in inequality. The state was for Marx an instrument of coercion permitting dominant social classes to subjugate peasants and the emerging working class to the needs of the wealthy or the bourgeoisie. This was all the more true in the case of colonial states bent on what Marx in 1867 termed 'primitive capitalist accumulation', or the conquest of land and resources at the global periphery (Marx 1976). From this point of view, the development of the state from an absolutist form to a democratic one over the course of the eighteenth and nineteenth centuries did not alter its function: the promotion of the interests of the dominant class. On the contrary, as Marx put it in 1848, it merely better disguised the function of the state as an instrument of class war and our representatives as 'a committee for managing the common affairs of the whole bourgeoisie' (Marx 1988: 57). Thus there is a curious symmetry between the views of the critics of representative democracy, such as Marx and Engels, and liberals such as Mill. Each agreed that the manner by which representative practices evolved in Europe and beyond promoted the dominant economic class as representatives of the interests of ordinary people. However, whereas Marx was confident that bourgeois rule would be overthrown by the working class, Mill was equally confident in the capacity of middle-class elites to convince those below that the best means of promoting their own needs and interests was through mandating 'the wise' to rule on their behalf.

The rise of 'representative politics'

The advent of competitive elections and a widening suffrage in the eighteenth and nineteenth centuries in Europe and beyond changed the dynamic of representation in important ways. With competition came the possibility of a different model of representation usually, though not exclusively, based on the political party. Parties offered the possibility for representing individuals on the basis of several axes, principally *identities*, *ideologies* and *interests*. Often parties combined these three elements; but for our purposes it is useful to hold them apart to see what is implied in each.

Identities. The onset of modernity witnessed the creation of new identities, particularly new class identities. It also accentuated certain others – in particular, religious, national and regional identities. Many of them began to find an outlet in the political process as parties were formed to defend the needs and interests of particular parts of the population (Duverger 1959). This was an important development in that it helped to institutionalize competition between identities that might otherwise have caused a fracturing of society, possibly leading to its disintegration. Political parties performed a key role in managing the various divisions displayed in the course of modernization and nation state-building (Dalton 2002). The mere fact that a party existed to defend one's interests as, say, a member of the working class or a Protestant meant that energies that might have been directed at contesting the legitimacy of the system were directed into the electoral process rather than out on the streets. To paraphrase Chantal Mouffe, political parties helped mediate potentially 'antagonistic' divisions in society so that they became 'agonistic' ones, or divisions between those who can accept another's viewpoint without seeing it as a threat to their own (Mouffe 1993). On the other hand, it is worth remarking that the effect of 'identity politics' has in certain contexts turned politics into a zero-sum game that has threatened rather than underpinned a stable political order. Belgium's political parties, for example, are so much the product of differences in identity that their *political* differences become secondary to their function of representing the particular ethnic, linguistic and class grouping in question. The result is that 'politics' takes a back seat to bickering over the rival claims of each ethnicity for primacy in territorial terms.

Ideologies. With the waning of the Church, space opened up for ideologies offering a different conception of how we should live. The Enlightenment proved an immensely fertile period in terms of the articulation of different visions of society speaking to different sections of the population and indeed different identities. The French and American revolutions were each in their own way the product of ideologies, but also catalysts for the development and refinement of new ones. Soon after the end of the eighteenth century, political parties emerged whose aim was to compete for power with a view to transforming or promoting a particular image of the good life. The development of ideologies in turn privileged intellectuals in the political process, those who could represent the needs and interests of particular elements of society. Socialists, for example, offered a critique of the present world, combined with an account of a much better world where the working class would be justly rewarded for their labour, and where their needs and interests would prevail over those of capitalists, assuming the latter had not disappeared or been rendered obsolescent in the process of transforming society. Ideologies offered the image of a better world to come together with an account of how this world was to be created and by whom. Liberals and conservatives had of course other ideas, more or less firmly mapped. At stake in the battle for ideologies was no less than the fate of humanity and the particular vision of rationality it would enact.

Interests. Hobbes argued that the job of the state is to promote peace, and nothing else. It was easy then for him to make the case for seeing the sovereign as representing our needs and interests irrespective of the lack of means of making the sovereign accountable. Yet even as he was writing in the mid-seventeenth century, the tasks of the state were becoming more complex, leading to increased taxation, and thus increasing demand that public expenditure be justified and scrutinized. With roads to be built, armies to be paid for, transgressors to be punished, the tasks allotted to these demands grew. Not everyone shared the same view as far as these developments were concerned, and the notion of 'interest' became more vexed with greater demands being placed on the state.

The emergence of political parties permitted a debate in terms of the differing impact of these developments on different groups in society. Interests also provided some stickiness for party identification in contexts where ideological differences were less pronounced than implied above and identities had either yet to coalesce in ways that influenced political behaviour or expressed themselves beyond the ballot box. The difference between, for example, the US Democrats and Republicans is better understood in terms of *interests* than in terms of either ideologies or identities. Whilst both parties are supportive of liberal capitalism, each speaks to a variety of different interests, even if residues of former affiliations and affinities can be seen, as, for example, in the phenomenon of the Southern Democrats – a conservative rump which rejected the overtures of the Republicans owing to their association with the North in the Civil War. If we are looking for reasons why people vote Democrat or Labour over the Republicans, the Conservatives or the Liberals in Australia, it would be because of the identification of Labour and the Democrats with the interests of the poor and marginalized, as opposed to the better off.

Parties are from this point of view 'interest aggregators': they cater for the expression of the different interests in society, in turn enabling a meaningful choice to be presented to the electorate (Holliday et al. 2002). Indeed, with the decline of ideology and identity as factors shaping the preferences of individual voters, interest becomes a more important basis for thinking about who and what is represented in the political process. If the view begins to take hold that the political process only represents the interests of 'the 1%', then one can confidently predict trouble to follow.

The emergence of party-based democracy in modernizing contexts was on its own terms highly successful. It produced a means of mediating competing and conflicting demands on the state. Cleavages and divisions which might conceivably have boiled over into social unrest were given an outlet in terms of an organized process that helped to convince emerging interests and identities that with organization, hard work and discipline they would be able to exercise power. Of particular note is the advancement towards the end of the nineteenth century and into the early twentieth century of social democratic parties, that is, of parties seeking to represent the needs and interests of the working class and the poorest elements in society. Even Marxist commentators note that the evolution of a competitive party process in which the needs and interests of ordinary people could be represented is a crucial factor in explaining the relative stability of these political systems (Miliband 1969; Jessop 1982). Social democratic parties made enormous strides in terms of ensuring that the fruits of capitalist production did not remain exclusively amongst the wealthy and privileged, but rather underpinned the establishment of national health systems, the development of compulsory education, social housing and welfare provision, including pensions and social facilities. But the extension of the suffrage impacted parties generally, making them more aware of the need to reach out beyond narrow or sectional interests to win elections.

The development of party-based representative politics is a key factor explaining why many ordinary people engaged willingly and enthusiastically in electoral politics. Particularly in the three decades after the Second World War, representative democracies were marked by high levels of engagement. Political parties were the mainstay of this phase of evolution and enjoyed widespread support in their own communities. On the other hand, as early observers of this style of politics noted, party politics was not without its own drawbacks (Michels 1998). In particular we can note the following:

51

The privileged place of intellectuals. Even when created to further the interests of the working class or the very poorest elements of society, political parties were often created by a middle-class intelligentsia. The example of the first communist parties is instructive. Karl Marx was a journalist, albeit he was impoverished for most of his adult life and therefore dependent on the support of Friedrich Engels, a wealthy mill owner. There was nothing unusual about the middle class taking on the role of articulating visions for those below. Nearly all the great works of socialism and anarchism were written by middle-class intellectuals. It could hardly be otherwise when literacy was still growing and when it was only those with the means to do so who could spend time in contemplation as well as in activism. But the legacy was a paternalist stance towards those to be represented. The leadership of political movements and parties, particularly radical ones, often felt that they had a better grasp on the nature of social reality, the direction society was taking and thus the elements that should compose the political programme. Whilst many political parties experimented with forms of internal democracy, often, as in the wider electoral process, this meant competition amongst *party elites*, as opposed to the ordinary membership. Political parties were characterized by a division of labour between those who were involved in directing the party and those who engaged in lesser tasks, such as expanding the membership or producing literature. Political parties were themselves microcosms of a world in which the division of labour between social classes held sway.

The iron law. The purpose of the party is capturing power, and, once captured, maintaining it. It is on this basis that the sociologist Robert Michels, writing at the start of the twentieth century, observed what he termed 'the iron law of oligarchy' (Michels 1998). Michels argued that it is in the very nature of large organizations, including political parties, that power tends to become concentrated in the hands of a few. Large organizations quickly become bureaucratic. The only means of exercising some control and leadership over them is to concentrate power so as to achieve the tasks that the organization is set up to serve. The virtue of concentrating power is in terms of the efficiency and speed with which decisions can be made. If only a small number of people are involved in decision-making, this makes the process much simpler and more direct. Yet there is a price to be paid. This is that political parties became oligarchical, narrow and elitist, reinforcing the message to activists that their views are rather less important than the views of those 'at the top'. The paradox has always been most pronounced in relation to left-wing parties, who often advertise themselves as seeking greater equality or greater opportunities for citizens to participate in decision-making. Many such parties have hardly been paragons of equality or participation themselves, using the privileged function of intellectuals in generating the party 'line' as a means of locking others out of the process.

Output politics. Party politics does not rule out activism or participation in politics; rather, it channels it in a particular way, that is, in terms of support for and engagement in a large organization whose primary focus is the capture of power to deliver the particular vision to which it is committed. From this point of view, Nadia Urbinati is justified in asserting that representative politics is not, as is sometimes argued, the antonym of 'participatory' politics (Urbinati 2011). Clearly participation is needed in order to maintain party politics. On the other hand, not everyone wants to be involved in a political party, particularly given the features already noted in relation to the division of labour found within them. The criticism is that representative politics is *pacifying* in the sense that parties compete with promises of what it is that will be produced should they be elected to power. Representative politics is above all about outputs, or 'delivery' as it now tends to be termed. It is much less about *empowering* people to be actors in their own right and in terms of the contexts in which this might make the most sense, for example in the workplace. Politics becomes a matter of producing the 'goods', of 'pork barrelling', of paying someone or some group back for their support. The process of participating counts for less than the outcomes. As Harold Lasswell put it, politics becomes a grey matter of 'who gets what, when, how' (Lasswell 1936).

Representative politics has thus tended to consecrate a particular image of the political as the concern of the state and our representatives who go on to exercise state power on our behalf. Many argue that it could hardly be otherwise in large complex settings such as modern nation states. But we are looking for reasons here why representation might as a practice be a turn-off for citizens, and some clues are surely contained in the remarks above. Parties were born in conditions where many ordinary people were excluded from the political process, where functional illiteracy reigned and where the condition of possibility for making oneself heard was limited. They are the product of the modernizing process, of the functional division of labour and the aggregation of identities, ideologies and interests in response to it. They still are. Where, after all, do we see party-based democracy in all its early modernizing grandeur today? India, a vast multi-ethnic society where the very poor huddle in a misery that can be disabling in political terms (Hewitt 2007). If there is a 'natural habitat' for the political party, then it is in such conditions, that is, where there is limited potential for exercising choices, for mobilizing, for organizing to defend the interests of some against others. But as we shall see in the next chapter, modernization problematizes the equation in ways that undercut the claim of parties and other 'aggregators' of our interests.

From 'majoritarian' politics to the politics of minorities

Party-based representative politics, which is still the dominant form that representative politics takes in most contemporary democracies, succeeded in opening up the political process to contestation. The advent of elections implied an element of choice based on rotation and accountability of those in power. Political scientists like to imagine that the competitive electoral system of this kind guaranteed that everyone had a stake in it. And this has been true up to a point. The pattern in many democratic countries has been a rotation of power between the major parties, for example the Democrats and the Republicans in the US, Labour and the Conservative party in the UK, and the Socialists and various Republican parties in France. The very fact that power rotates in this fashion offers the impression of a healthy and dynamic system in which different ideologies and conceptions of society get their chance to engage the electorate. But it's an impression that owes a lot to the idea of a relatively homogeneous community in which the different values, viewpoints and opinions in society more or less accurately map onto the offerings of the available political parties. It's an impression with some purchase in contexts where the 'imagined community' of the nation has some sociological reality, and where the expression of political preferences follows the axes described above in terms of different identities, ideologies and interests. Yet what is becoming more apparent is that this narrative is being disrupted, in turn provoking reflection on how best to configure representative democracy and the practices associated with it. To take a few prominent examples:

Indigenous peoples. The process of decolonization over the course of the twentieth century had the effect of consecrating the existence of nation states whose borders were defined by historical accident as opposed to the existence of a more or less homogeneous nation or people. Representative democratic systems were created ensuring that a dominant or majority ethnicity held sway over various minority groups that happened to find themselves within the relevant territorial borders. This was particularly the case for indigenous peoples, who were in many cases overrun by settlers and new migrants (Fleras and Elliott 1992). Thus even where indigenous people were granted political rights, they often found themselves without effective representation on the basis that their numbers were too few to count in electoral terms. Indigenous peoples in countries like Australia have found themselves in the position of being marginalized from the political process and placed in a position of extreme vulnerability as far as their own way of life and access to resources are concerned. Different countries have found different mechanisms to overcome the marginalizing effects of 'majoritarian' democracy. Some political systems such as New Zealand guarantee a certain representation for indigenous peoples within national assemblies (Gallagher and Mitchell 2005). Other systems offer more or less autonomy to indigenous peoples to arrange matters to their own advantage in designated territories or reserves. Both have their defenders, and also their detractors, both within such communities and without. On the other hand, what the case highlights is that the pluralist model of representation according to identities, ideologies and interests only carries one so far before it comes up against the inheritance of colonialism in many parts of the world. It also highlights why certain groups, such as the Zapatistas, choose to turn their back on electoral politics altogether in favour of some variety or other of 'autonomous politics' beyond the clutches of federal authorities. They're not interested in power, and nor do they have the numbers to make themselves 'count'. Self-exile to their own communities and way of life is therefore a logical response to the majoritarian logic of representative systems.

Multiculturalism. A different set of issues is posed by another facet of decolonization, which is the inflow of people into the metropolitan space from the colonial periphery. The arrival of those with a minoritarian identity poses new issues in terms of recognition and representation (Kymlicka 2001). Different countries have adopted different mechanisms for recognizing the existence of migrant identities – or not. France, for example, remains resolutely wedded to its republican model of citizenship in which individuals are seen as first and foremost 'French'. 'Minority' demands are contained, that is, until they explode, forcing some recognition of the reality that 'Frenchness' is a far from homogeneous category. Elsewhere, as in the UK, it is common to hear talk of different 'communities', with the implication that they should be permitted to opt out of certain practices: for example, it was argued that Sikhs should be able to opt out of wearing motorcycle helmets on account of their turbans (Parekh 2002). The difficulty again is finding ways in which the political process can be made responsive to minority demands where the electoral logic places them at a disadvantage to the majority ethnic group. Recognizing the existence of different communities can have an empowering effect. However, it can also send the signal that 'community leaders', often self-appointed, are given *carte blanche* to arrange the affairs of their own 'community' to their own tastes. The fear is that they create ghettos in which, for example, young women are expected to adopt the pattern of behaviour of their mothers and grandmothers, thereby denying them opportunities available to young women of the dominant ethnicity. 'Representation' here may thus suffocate possibilities for members of these communities as opposed to guaranteeing them some voice and sense of possibility.

Marginal or 'minor' politics. The logic of electoral politics can serve to narrow the spectrum of political choices rather than to expand it in ways that may facilitate the representation of different views. Political parties exist to win elections, and to win elections they usually seek to appeal to the broadest range of voters. This often makes them small 'c' conservative in terms of their own strategy and message. The effect politically can be to squeeze out positions, viewpoints and opinions that don't fit. At the same time this means that those with heterodox, critical, unfashionable, radical or in some way or other minoritarian tastes in politics find themselves left behind in the rush for the 'centre ground'. Too bad, one may think; but this can mean the closing down of democratic discourse and by extension the sense that the views of ordinary citizens count. A range of views and opinions find themselves unrepresented, without a voice, and thus without a stake in the political system. Historically, 'minor' viewpoints have been able to assemble themselves under the banner of social movements, for example around the environment, climate change, the advancement of otherwise marginalized or ignored segments of the population, those contesting 'neoliberalism', and so forth. In an electorally based system of representation such movements find themselves on the outside of a process looking in, having to resort to lobbying, direct action, marches and protests. This itself poses questions in terms of representation. How effective are such movements in getting their message across? How representative or how democratic are these movements themselves, particularly in comparison to political parties? How should democracy treat the claims of those seeking to represent people who for whatever reason are unable or unwilling to make their claims subject to the electoral process?

Conclusion

Surveying in whistle-stop fashion the various iterations of representation and representative politics as these have unfolded over modernity, the overall impression we get is of a relatively simple relation, that between Hobbes's sovereign and the people, that gives way to successively more complex iterations of the representative process. We move from the pluralism of the one, the multitude, coming together to create a singular relationship with the sovereign, to the pluralism of different identities, ideologies and interests, to the pluralism of the many. But even this iteration is itself disrupted by the emergence of new identities and demands that cannot be encapsulated readily within the apparatus of party-based democracy. New kinds of organization are created in order to advance these demands to a point where we are confronted not only with a plurality of demands, but also with a plurality of ways in which demands are articulated within and beyond the representative or electoral system itself. Mike Saward claims with good reason that it now makes little sense to talk about representative politics as a matter of certain individuals who do the representing; rather it is a question of representative *claims* articulated within and without the formal system of representation (Saward 2010).

Notwithstanding its capacity to morph and change with the times, representative politics has been anchored in certain features of the modern landscape: the birth of the nation state; the creation of aggregate identities and interests which can then be represented; a sense of possibility created by a political system claiming sovereign authority over a given territory; notions of power as a singular resource that can be possessed, captured and used for better ends. These are all aspects of the modern imagination. So too is the idea of the functional division of labour, of the inevitability, if not desirability, that some will rule or govern, and others will follow.

Representative politics is in this sense a politics of *disjuncture* that is firmly rooted in the experience of modernity: the disjuncture between the state and society, between elites and ordinary people, between rich states and poor states, between party leaders and those whose identity or interests they seek to represent (Hardt and Negri 2004). The not so hidden premise of representative politics is that the element to be represented (class, nation, people) cannot govern, manage, lead itself, and so must be governed, managed, led. Such a notion, intuitive as it may seem, has historically permitted a certain dynamic to underpin the self-understanding of representative politics. Because we cannot govern, lead, rule ourselves, *then someone or some group must be found who can.* The question has always been posed in terms not of *why*, but of who and how? Whom shall we entrust to represent us? How do we ensure that they remain true to that mission? How do we protect ourselves from those who lead or govern? This has for two hundred years or so been the stock in trade of thinking about politics, with some exceptions, as we have seen. But what is becoming clearer is that the growing alienation from representative practices and processes is moving us beyond the 'who' and 'how' questions towards the 'why'.

— 3 —

ARE WE BECOMING
UNREPRESENTABLE?

In the previous chapter we sought to locate representation and representative politics in a historical context. Representation is, we found, a discourse associated with modernity and the creation of nation states. As modernity develops, so the connotations attached to representation and representative politics alter. From being the description of a relationship serving the purpose of absolutist rulers, representation quickly evolves into a way of thinking about a mechanism for mediating between the state and the People or civil society. The mechanism of mediation itself undergoes several important mutations to arrive at the party-based form of representative politics so familiar today. Representation by political parties is not the only way in which citizens come to be represented, but it is still the key to unlocking the operation of democracy in most parts of the world. It's a formula that was seen by many commentators as underpinning the success and stability of representative democracies over the past century or so.

Today the picture looks bleaker. Political scientists huddle together in conferences with titles such as 'Representation & Renewal' and 'Is the Party Over?' seeking a panacea for the ills of representative politics.[1] Many alight on short-term or contingent factors, with the hope, if not the expectation, that addressing these issues will 'renew' representative politics. Others, as already noted, are less sanguine, seeing the decline in the practice and profile of representative politics as rooted in deeper or longer-term changes of an irreversible kind. Some are even more pessimistic than this, declaring representative democracy to be in danger of expiring (*Can Democracy Be Saved?* – Della Porta 2013), assuming that it is not already dead (*The Life and Death of Democracy* – Keane 2009).

In this chapter we look at some of the dominant explanations for the crisis. Many understandably alight on short-term or contingent factors to analyse the symptoms of crisis. However, as implied in the summary from the previous chapter, I think we need to look to the underlying transformation of contemporary society for causes. We are moving from societies marked by strong collective identities, ideologies and interests, which in turn form the basis for political parties and other forms of representation, to societies marked by a resistance to representation and representative politics. This does not in and of itself suggest the *death* of representation or representative democracy, more its transformation as a setting for a different political dynamic. Working our way through some of the explanations will thus provide a useful backdrop for the later discussion in which I try to say how these changes are playing out and what they mean or imply for our understanding of democracy.

Why is representative politics in crisis?

The contemporary crisis of representation elicits a number of imaginative and thoughtful explanations from political commentary. Thinking about the different kinds of explanation on offer, three stand out: (1) the crisis as stemming from the decadence or failure of the political class; (2) the crisis as stemming from the changing behaviour or comportment of citizens; and (3) the crisis as the product of neoliberalism and the transformation of the role and image of the state.

The problem with politicians . . .

Many commentators see the decline in interest in politics as closely linked to what they perceive to be the decline in the standing of politicians in the eyes of the public (Burchell and Leigh 2002; Goot 2002; Riddell 2010). It's a good place to start. The heyday of representative politics in the middle of the twentieth century correlates with the high standing of politicians. At this point the term 'politician' equated to the idea of 'public servant', and by extension someone whose primary interest was in serving the community rather than advancing his or her own position. Politics was still at this juncture permeated by the paternalist ethos that we were discussing in the previous chapter. Elites were often raised with an expectation that they should seek some way of being of use to the wider community, and 'public service' as a representative was regarded as a noble calling or 'vocation'.

60

The professionalization of politics over the course of the twentieth century, and in particular the paying of a salary to members of Parliament or Congress, is seen as changing this perception in important ways. Politics attracted a different kind of individual, not just quasi-aristocratic figures with the means and time to attend to the welfare of the nation, but those who might have worked their way up through a trade union or professional association. Payment meant a greater emphasis on the accountability of politicians. It also prompted the development of a transactional mindset in electors (*well I pay for them, what have they done for me?*), in turn diluting some of the deference previously attached to the political class. This encouraged the press and media to peer more closely into the lives of representatives, with the justification that as paid employees of the state there was a public interest in ensuring their integrity and honesty. Scandals such as the 1962 Profumo Affair, in which a British Cabinet Minister became involved with a topless dancer also rumoured to be involved with a Russian spy, set the tone, at least in UK. Tales of the sordid underbelly of politics attracted increased attention and sales of newspapers, but at the cost of the standing of the political class (Thompson 2000; Heywood and Krastev 2006).

Today, it is almost impossible for politicians to escape the gaze of the 24/7 media, and yet the scandals flow in what in certain contexts can seem like a torrent of decadent behaviour, whether in the form of sexual affairs (Bill Clinton, Antony Weiner, John Edwards), infidelities (François Hollande) or 'romps' (John Major, Ron Brown, Mark Oaten), the fathering of illegitimate children (François Mitterrand), financial impropriety (the Bettencourt Affair, UK MPs' expenses scandal), corruption (Eddie Obeid, Jacques Chirac, Jack Abramoff, Spiro Agnew), lewd behaviour (Silvio Berlusconi), spying (Watergate, Clearstream) or callous disregard for the lives or reputations of others (the David Kelly Inquiry, the Francis J. Harvey scandal, Chappaquiddick). Every new story provokes a fresh sense of indignation at the affairs, literal and figurative, of the political class. Movements such as those of the *Indignados*, the Iceland 'revolution' and Occupy are as much a product of disgust or anger at the behaviour of the political class as they are at the financial austerity, hardship or difficulty caused by bureaucrats and bankers. Politicians have, it seems, lost the plot, leading to our alienation from actual and would-be guardians of the public interest. The crisis of representation is at one level a crisis located in the failure of our representatives to convince us that they should be trusted and respected.

There's a lot to be said for this line of explanation, not least because

it chimes with recent data that show strong support for the institutions of democracy such as the police and the legal system, but alienation from politicians and political parties (Newton and Norris 2000).
A gulf seems to be opening up in many democratic countries between
ordinary citizens and the political class. This in turn helps make sense
of the rise of a certain kind of *anti*-politician who through his or her
very ordinariness, plain words and outsider status is able to ride the
tide of this disaffection. In the wake of corruption scandals in Spain,
to take one example we will be coming back to, two popular figures
have emerged symbolizing the desire for a different kind of leader:
Ada Colau, the tough-talking spokeswoman for the popular campaign against evictions (see Chapter 5), and Sister Teresa Forcades,
'Europe's most radical nun', whose homespun 'anti-capitalism' and
unimpeachable integrity resonates far beyond church-goers.[2] And
there are many others. Evo Morales, President of Bolivia, trades
on his lack of ostentation, sporting a colourful woven jumper on
public occasions instead of the usual business suit. He follows in
the line of ascetic, self-denying or humble figures such as Gandhi,
Havel, Mandela and Walesa. More worrying is the march of populist
figures such as Sarah Palin, Marine Le Pen and Nigel Farage who
style themselves 'one of us', 'ordinary' folks fed up with the excesses
of the political class, keen to get back to ordinary decent values and
'common sense'. The fear is that figures such as these will tap into
the well-spring of discontent with representative politics to pursue
an agenda that might *worsen* democratic engagement and public
discourse rather than address it in a positive and constructive way.
They are to politics what 'shock jocks' and shrieking bumper stickers
are to informed public debate. They seek instant solutions to complex
problems, whether it be immigration or resource depletion. The rise
of populism and populist figures is in this sense less a panacea for the
decline of representative politics than a symptom *of* crisis (Moffitt
2014).

So is the decline of the political class really the cause of the
problem? It's certainly *part* of the problem, particularly as regards
the erosion of trust, which, as we noted, is a key indicator in terms
of the crisis, but to see the decline of voting, membership of political
parties and interest in politics as a result of the collective decadence of
politicians is stretching the point. The rejection of politicians clearly
goes beyond a sense of exasperation with the mannerisms and gestures of the political class and embraces the very idea at the heart of
representation, that some should be elevated to a position of power
whilst everyone else is placed in the position of passive spectators,

the represented. Representation implies a politics in which some act, engage, direct, lead, and the rest follow, in turn mimicking some of the more alienating aspects of contemporary life that many such initiatives are seeking to query: the seeming powerlessness of ordinary people to have a say in the world around them.

Reflecting on initiatives such as the *Indignados* and Occupy, a key feature has been the creation of assemblies with elaborate mechanisms to encourage the participation of as many people as possible. It is why the World Social Forum was constituted as a 'space for dialogue' and why protests and demonstrations against the G8 and G20 are accompanied by 'convergence zones' in which different groups and initiatives can share their experiences and generate proposals together. In short, where once the powerlessness of ordinary people pointed at the *need* for representatives, intellectuals, leaders, politicians, to represent them, the tables seem to be turning. At some level the figure of the politician has come to represent *loss* of the power to act and speak for oneself. This is partly a question of inheritance, and the perceived failure of 'leader-centred' politics to provide a successful template in many parts of the world, but also partly a question of need. We are, it seems, becoming resistant to others speaking in our name – and that is what politicians do for a living.

The problem with citizens . . .

If it's not politicians or our representatives who are to blame for the crisis, then logically it seems it must be us, the citizens. Ronald Inglehart offers a useful starting point for this angle of analysis in his analysis of the 'post-materialist' comportment of the contemporary citizen (Inglehart 1990). His view is that, such has been the success of democratic society in providing relative affluence, access to welfare, education, that citizens have come to take all of this for granted. After decades of rising living standards we have become complacent, apathetic, unmoved by politics. Matthew Flinders shares the view that citizens must shoulder some of the blame, but writes in terms of the unreasonable expectations that give rise to discontent (Flinders 2012). We have become ensnared in the false promise of more services and benefits for less taxation, blaming politicians when things go wrong, as they inevitably must, given the nature of the equation. Flinders urges greater realism in terms of our judgement of politicians, whom he sees as by and large hard-working and indeed public-spirited individuals. We need, as he puts it, 'to grow up' (Flinders 2012: 39).

Elsewhere commentators such as Zygmunt Bauman bemoan the

emergence of a narcissistic self-absorbed culture that focuses on personal lifestyle as opposed to matters of public concern (Bauman 2001). From this point of view, it should hardly be surprising that we find engagement in representative processes in decline. Politics by its nature asks us to think about the common or collective interest, as opposed to how one is going to 'feel good' or 'get ahead'. So preoccupied have we become with our own advancement or amusement that we have lost the will to take part in the affairs of the common.

There's no doubt a good deal of truth in these explanations. It certainly seems to be the case that part of the reason why voting and engagement are in decline is a deep sense of apathy amongst the electorate. Apathy can, as Inglehart suggests, be a sign of relative contentment, a sign that by and large things are working fine and that therefore I don't need to pay much attention to what is going on around me: *let them get on with it*. Apathy can be the shrug of those who feel that life is ticking along quite nicely and that therefore there is little incentive to get involved, or make the short trip to the polling station. Apathy of this kind is nonetheless an irritant to political commentary. It undermines the idea that the legitimacy of the system stems from the *active consent* of citizens, and their engagement in the key processes that enable the system to reproduce itself, namely elections. An indifferent public is hardly the basis for celebration if one's view is that representative democracy is the pinnacle of political development – 'the end of history' no less.

Apathy can, however, also have its root in more negative feelings. It may be based on a feeling that my view or vote counts for very little, that politicians don't care about what I think: *What do they care about me?* Or, as the title of ex-Mayor of London Ken Livingstone's book puts it, *If Voting Changed Anything, They'd Abolish It* (Livingstone 1987). Political scientists are also attentive to such signs and signals from citizens, not least because they can be measured, compared, weighed and sifted over time and across systems – as in the much-quoted 'Euro-barometer' data that measure the well-being and contentment of the Euro-citizenry with their political systems.[3] As a result there's a lively debate about, for example, the design of electoral systems. The question is often posed in the specialist literature as to whether certain systems are better able to offer the impression to citizens that their vote counts (Cox 1997; Farrell 1997). Political scientists are also interested in studying the effects of different kinds of initiative in sparking the interest of ordinary citizens. Hence the burgeoning literature on participatory experiments, citizenship initiatives of all kinds, e-democracy, citizenship education, and so on

(Smith 2009). The hope is that with some tweaks here and minor reforms there apathy can be banished, citizens re-engaged and representative politics renewed. Yet for all the interest in such initiatives, some handsomely funded from central governments, the impact in terms of the overall story of the decline of engagement and participation in mainstream politics is at best uncertain, and at worst negligible (Rosanvallon 2011: Ch.12). Indeed the launch of yet another initiative to 're-engage citizens' often has the whiff of rearranging the deckchairs on the *Titanic*, as opposed to showing us how the *Titanic* will avoid the looming iceberg.

Not all citizens are apathetic, of course. Many note the emergence of 'critical citizens' using non-mainstream and non-electoral means to make themselves heard, from the humble practice of letter writing and organizing petitions, to demonstrations, protests and large-scale mobilizations (Norris 1999). Much of this activity can look like a *supplement* to mainstream and official politics. It doesn't replace official politics, and nor does it threaten it. On the contrary, it might be said that it gives greater legitimacy to mainstream politics because it deepens democratic engagement rather than altering or contesting it. It is for this reason that political scientists are often enthusiastic about promoting 'participation', particularly when they can see a flow-on effect in terms of bolstering political parties, and increasing the number of citizens voting. One example of this kind of supplementary participation is GetUp!, which seeks to encourage young people in Australia to get involved in politics through campaigning on a range of causes. It's motivated by the perception that the young have become apathetic about politics, and thus need to be encouraged to assert their voice on issues of 'progressive' concern.[4] GetUp! is one of the great success stories of contemporary Australian politics, attracting around 700,000 members, more than the membership of the Labour and Liberal parties combined, if with lower entry costs. Another success story, though a global one, is Avaaz.org, which similarly seeks to identify causes and issues of interest to the young, albeit internationally rather than nationally.[5] Avaaz generates petitions and actions with the intention of shaming elites into action. It claims a number of notable successes, including highlighting instances of corruption in Brazil and lobbying for safety legislation to protect Bangladeshi garment workers in the wake of the collapse of a clothing factory. And there are legions of other similar organisations: MoveOn.org, change.org, 38 degrees, and so on, allowing those with access to the internet and some sense of collective concern to 'get active'. Sort of.

This may well look encouraging to those who want to read citizen activism as a sign of a healthy and vibrant democratic culture. Yet the rise of disaffiliated activism (activism beyond or outside political parties), protests and direct action has yet to correlate with a revival of political parties and a renewed interest in voting. Quite the opposite: it has been accompanied by a decline of party membership and a deepening disinterest in mainstream politics. The enormous increase in, for example, environmental activism has not resulted in a massive uptake of the membership of Green parties. Nor, with a few honourable exceptions, has it seen a significant breakthrough of Green parties into the mainstream or national government. Environmental activism has, on the contrary, remained disaggregated, unaffiliated for the most part, localized, sporadic, or what activists sometimes term 'dis-organized', indicating a style or form of activism that self-consciously rejects the bureaucratic, hierarchical and passive mode of activism associated rightly or wrong with political parties (Anderson 2004). Similarly, the emergence of a Global Justice Movement in the wake of the Seattle protests has not so far provided the launch-pad for the reinvigoration of left parties. Rather, as we noted in Chapter 1, the more eye-catching institutional innovations of the Global Justice Movement have been studiously and self-consciously anti-representational, anti-electoral and anti-party, certainly at the level of its own discourse.

What the above discussion signals is the danger of reading every instance of activism as 'participation', with the implication that this will lead to the renewal of representative politics. If anything, the opposite would seem to be the case as citizens begin to flex their muscles and work out that organizing from outside the mainstream is becoming easier, and that relatively spontaneous mass actions can offer a way of making oneself heard outside or beyond traditional representative bodies such as trade unions and political parties. Certainly the recent emergence of mass mobilizations, occupations, demonstrations, in countries as diverse as the US, Spain, Turkey and Brazil is a wake-up call to those who seek to make the connection between the emergence of activist citizens and support for existing processes and institutions. The image we are left with in events such as these is not 'participation' or joining in, but anger against the political class, the political system, representatives of whatever stripe. The latter point is, predictably, a frustration to left intellectuals who urge the formulation of political demands, and the construction of a new party able to represent the needs and interests of the alienated and fed-up (Dean 2009). But the resistance to incorporation into a political project is what has come to define insurgent grassroots poli-tics. Resistance to politicians, programmes, ideologies, is at one level *what they are about.*

The problem with neoliberalism . . .

Other kinds of explanation for the crisis of representation focus on the larger processes shaping the climate within which politics is taking place. Colin Hay, for example, argues that much of the blame for our growing disillusionment with politics and politicians stems from the emergence of neoliberalism and the New Public Management to undermine the welfare state (Hay 2007). It's no coincidence that the height of our involvement in mainstream politics in the 1950s and 1960s coincided with the emergence of the social democratic con-sensus and the establishment of the welfare state in many advanced democracies. In the post-war period, advanced democracies greatly extended the importance and centrality of the state in terms of organ-izing the economy, providing employment and a range of services and entitlements to ordinary citizens. The state occupied a central role in people's lives, one that encouraged and facilitated their engagement in the electoral process. However the 'crisis of the welfare state' of the late 1970s and early 1980s led to the questioning of this inherit-ance and the election of those such as Thatcher and Reagan who were dedicated to combating collectivism. The overall effect was to *depoliticize* the public sector, leading to a loss of the sense of the state as promoting a vision of the public good or public interest. As Hay and others argue, since politicians are themselves complicit in the devaluing of the public realm, it should hardly be surprising that we hold them in increasing contempt and want to turn our back on the processes that mandate them. With nowhere to go, voters preferred to turn off rather than tune in.

There's a lot to be said for Hay's analysis, but there are also some puzzles. Firstly, neoliberalism didn't arrive out of thin air and implant itself behind the backs of unsuspecting citizens. Difficult though it may be to swallow for progressive academics, Thatcher, Reagan, Bush, Howard, Blair ('Son of Thatcher'), all won multiple elections. They did so by convincing a lot of ordinary citizens that their own interests would be best served by cutting taxes, public services and the welfare state. Dare one say it, but neoliberalism was a *popular* as well as populist political movement. It appealed to certain ambitions and aspirations, principally freedom from state control, from increasing taxes, indeed from *politicians*. In this sense neoliberalism is not only a cause of a general malaise with politics and politicians, it's also an *effect* of it. The rhetorical appeal of neoliberalism lies in appealing to individual freedom as opposed to collectivism ('the nanny state'), personal responsibility as opposed to state entitlement; and promising that politicians will cease telling us 'what to do'. This chimed. And it won elections.

What about the other side of the coin? If our reason for 'hating' politics or politicians is because the latter have given up on collectivism, the public realm and the positive role of the state in underpinning public services, then we might expect parties or groups that opposed or contested neoliberalism to grow in support or at least remain relatively unaffected. By and large, however, this has not been the case, certainly not in the advanced democracies. In the developing world there has certainly been a reaction along these lines, as the election of Hugo Chávez in Venezuela, Lula da Silva in Brazil and the Pink Tide phenomenon in Latin America testifies. But in Europe, for example, the picture looks rather different. Even in countries such as France, Spain and Italy where far left parties have enjoyed considerable support within recent memory, the left remains at best a stagnant political force. Rather than garnering support amongst those disaffected with neoliberal policies, we see the fragmentation of parties and waning interest amongst the young. Where there has been an impact is in terms of generating interest and support for initiatives such as the Global Justice Movement and the World Social Forum, both framed by activists participating in them as 'contesting neoliberalism'. And yet even a modest proposal to generate a political organization that might give an outlet to people's frustrations (the Bamako Appeal led by Samir Amin and François Houtart) fell on stony ground. Indeed the popularity of both initiatives increased in direct proportion to the degree to which they distanced themselves from the inheritance of left-wing party politics as that has been practised for a century and a half. Strange days.

The long revolution: modernity, globalization, individualization

As Hay and others sharing this analysis acknowledge, the story of the emergence of neoliberalism is also a story about changes in the composition of social and political life in modern societies. To get to the root of the crisis of representation we need to dig deeper to touch on the changes that are impacting the political field. The chief change for our purposes lies in the transition from societies based on firm collective identities to those based on a much more complex mix of identities and post-identities that resist easy reformulation in political terms.

As we noted in the previous chapter, representative politics works when people recognize themselves as members of some larger aggregate grouping: 'the working class', 'the British people', 'the battlers'. As we also noted, political parties came about to represent the needs and interests of certain key identities. Their success was built on their ability to connect to those sharing the identity. But as many social theorists have argued, the ground or basis for the development of collective identities is ebbing under the pressure of processes connected with the transformation of contemporary society. Different terms are used to describe these changes. Some sociologists argue for a clear 'break' between, for example, 'first' and 'second' modernity, or between 'modernity' and 'postmodernity'. Whether it is possible to identify a clear moment when one kind of contemporary society gave way to another is less important for our purposes than establishing what the natures of the changes are that are said to have disrupted or altered the nature of politics, identity and the manner of interactions between citizens. The key changes are these: (1) the transition from Fordism to Post-Fordism; (2) transnationalism and deterritorialization; and (3) communicative abundance.

The transition from 'Fordism' to 'Post-Fordism'

According to social theorists such as David Harvey, Anthony Giddens and Zygmunt Bauman, the key to understanding many of the other changes in the composition of contemporary social and political life is the transformation of the basis of the contemporary economy (Harvey 1989; Giddens 1991; Bauman 1998). Advanced economies are moving away from traditional forms of production, from manufacturing, agriculture and mining towards 'the service economy'. Traditional employment built around a local factory or mine is being displaced by work in banking, finance, IT and insurance, the creative industries, through various styles of office employment, to work in call centres, shopping centres and retail parks. At the same time, employment is becoming more 'flexible', meaning that workers are now expected and sometimes required to move, be adaptable and develop skills consonant with the underlying shifts in the nature of the economy.

Flexibility often equates to greater 'precarity' for workers as the pattern of 9–5, 'job for life' employment gives way to much higher levels of casualization, contract- and fee-based work, work without the entitlements and benefits associated with traditional employment such as sick leave, pensions and holiday pay. The developments have significant knock-on effects in terms of the pattern of social and family life, the relationship between the sexes and between generations. Whereas in previous generations individuals had an expectation of living and working in the same town or region for most of their lives, now many of us can expect to move in search of promotion, better employment, or because the employer has shut down, merged or moved its operations elsewhere. The nature of employment has also changed in important ways. The shift away from production towards services leads to a shift away from the performance of manual tasks, often of a repetitive or routine kind, towards forms of intellectual and 'affective' labour as manual skills give way to skills in selling, dealing with clients, negotiating, organizing. The new forms of labour are increasingly based on reduced face-to-face direction, but often at the price of a 'performance'- or 'results'-based regime that valorizes the individual contribution through bonuses, rewards, accelerated promotion, and the like.

Many of the elements that generated a sense of class identity and class solidarity are thus eroding as traditional forms of work give way to individualized, knowledge- and performance-based forms of work. Under Fordist conditions, people were identified by the job that they did, and most of those jobs readily defined one either as a worker or as a manager. There was deep awareness of the distinction, what it meant and what the politics of the categories implied. Working in a factory or down a mine defined one as 'working class', and there would have been few factory workers or miners who saw themselves on any other terms. There was a certain clarity about where one stood in terms of the social hierarchy. This was reinforced by the fact that working-class people tended to live in the same area in similar conditions, wearing similar clothes, eating similar food and undertaking similar activities during their leisure time. The concept of 'the working class' had a sociological reality. The emergence of a self-identifying working class in turn gave impetus to a politics built on class identity. When the Labour Party was created in Britain in 1900, there would have been few who doubted what it was for or whom it represented. The same applies for the communist, socialist and social democratic parties that emerged in the latter half of the nineteenth century and the early twentieth century. Class was a key – and in some contexts *the* key – marker of political identity.

Today the picture looks rather different – certainly in many advanced democracies, if not at the global 'periphery' where many manufacturing jobs have ended up and where the cycle of working-class militancy is often still evident. But in the most advanced economies the shift from manual labour towards varieties of 'affective' labour has clouded the matter. The neat distinctions between those who toiled and those who cracked the whip have been replaced by finer-grained distinctions of seniority and differentiated 'skill sets'. Even those distinctions that exist can blur as those at the 'top' affect the mannerisms of those at the bottom, and vice versa. The media delight in tracing the decline of social distinctions, from the erosion of distinctive class accents ('estuary English' etc.), and the predominance of 'fashion' over the distinctive styles once associated with social position, to the taking over of working-class sport by the middle class, and of middle-class pursuits by the *nouveax riche*. A recent report on social class in the UK argued that the old tripartite division of classes (working, middle, upper) had been replaced by a more fluid seven-layer system based on a large number of contingent variables as opposed to caste-like permanent markings of position within the hierarchy.[6]

Class has not therefore disappeared. However, it does not provide the clarity in terms of interests it once did. As Ulrich Beck comments in *The Risk Society*, 'we increasingly confront the phenomenon of capitalism without classes, but with individualized social inequality and all the related social and political problems' (Beck 1992: 88). Marx's expectation that we would see a *polarization* of the class system in advance of a final showdown between the proletariat and bourgeoisie has not so far materialized in sociological terms, even if there are occasional hints of it in political terms. Occupy's evoking of 'the 99%' pitted against 'the 1%' *does* speak to such a polarization, but the avoidance of the term 'class' in the discourse of Occupy and similar initiatives is eye-catching. It's as if mere mention of the 'c' word conjures up all manner of associations that might upset the tenor of what activists are seeking to achieve. 'Class politics' is, it seems, too redolent of a certain style of enacting politics that activists are trying to get away from: a politics where representatives of the working class speak and act on behalf of workers, leaving the latter as passive onlookers. So the irony is that at the moment when the idea of a numerically tiny group (the 1%) ripping everyone else off (the 99%) seems to chime for many, the vocabulary that might best explain that phenomenon and prepare the way for a political response seems off-limits, obsolescent.

Transnational flows and deterritorialization

A key feature of contemporary life is the increased flow of people, culture, ideas. Migration can be traced to a number of different factors, including the intensification of conflicts at the global periphery producing a stream of would-be and actual migrants seeking greater security. This is conjoined by economic migration amongst the poor and unemployed looking for work, and also amongst wealthier citizens seeking to take advantage of the global market for high-level skills and experience. The effects are particularly pronounced in the metropolitan centres, in turn changing the geographies of the contemporary world. As Saskia Sassen has documented, we are seeing the emergence of 'global cities' such as London, Paris, Toronto, Mumbai and Sydney which attract huge numbers of new migrants seeking work and a better life (Sassen 2006). This in turn produces a shift in the nature of the relationship between the rural and the urban, between agricultural workers and new socio-economic groupings, indeed between the nation and the international, on the one hand, and the city on the other. These vast cosmopolitan settings are at the cutting edge of globalization and the mixing and *métissage* of cultures that is such a feature of contemporary life.

The accelerating flows of peoples around the world would seem to be highly disruptive of received and inherited identities. Where once identity was rooted in the security of a community in which one lived, worked, grew up, got married, had children, increasing mobility unanchors identity as something fixed, determinate and 'known'. Mobility makes identity less certain. Identity has to be reconstructed, renegotiated, rethought. Some go further and argue that mobility makes for new identities as individuals encounter each other in the metropolitan spaces where new migrants, rich and poor, tend to find themselves. New or 'hybrid' identities proliferate on the back of the interaction of different communities, peoples, nations, ethnicities, poured into the melting pot of the mega-city (Bhabha 1994). Of course, certain identities are less negotiable than others. Only someone with a white face such as myself could possibly imagine that racial identity is something negotiated or capable of redescription. One doesn't chose one's race, and one doesn't choose how others see one's race. But other components of identity are increasingly up for grabs. They are a source of many of the dilemmas and conflicts at the heart of modern life, particularly as younger migrants deal with the demands of their own 'community' at the same time as fitting in with the complex and multiform nature of the context they find themselves in.

What this narrative reveals is the problematic inheritance of nationalism and the idea of the self-determination of peoples, which, as we noted in the previous chapter, is the cornerstone of representative politics as that has been understood over the past two and a half centuries. Nations are 'imagined communities', self-identifying collectivities marked by a common purpose and some sort of ethos that unites those sharing a particular identity (Anderson 2006). Take that away and we are left with an increasingly random assortment of individuals sharing territory, not community. Hence the increasingly frantic efforts of states to feed the imagined community of nations and peoples through ever more elaborate national days of celebration, citizenship ceremonies, language requirements and all the paraphernalia of complex post-nationalism such as the creation of 'multicultural patriotism' (Soutphommasane 2009). However, the sense of the state, political parties or other representative bodies as being able to represent this increasingly disparate assemblage of cultures and (non-) identities wanes as the velocity of interactions increases.

The proliferation of information, media, communication

Knowledge used to be the preserve of the Church, the state and elites. Those who could read and write exerted great power over those who could not ('the represented'), not least because the latter were dependent on the former for their knowledge of the world. That relationship has changed dramatically with the spread of literacy, the proliferation of knowledge sources and latterly the internet revolution, which potentially at least opens up not just knowledge acquisition, but knowledge *creation*. A couple of generations ago our major source of understanding of the world came from a small number of often state-owned TV channels and a handful of broadsheet newspapers. The internet and social networking technologies alter the nature and form of communication between citizens and between citizens and elites. They accelerate the flow of images, news, opinion and of interactions between people, groups and organizations.

All this said, communication is not 'democratized' so much as *multiplied* and *intensified* as the flow from all manner of sources increases. There are many more opportunities to produce media and to select media according to one's whim or need. Such is the force of the flow that commentators sometimes conclude that it must be the trivial, the eye-catching and the scandalous that gain the upper hand, squeezing out media of a considered, detailed or complex character (Bauman 1987). And by and large they're not wrong; but at the same time the ability of individuals and groups to broadcast themselves over YouTube, Twitter and Facebook changes the dynamic of news creation as well as its reception. There's a lively debate about the role of social media in events such as the Arab Spring and the Turkish occupations, but what seems undeniable is that without social media these events would have unfolded in a very different way (Morozov 2012). The scales are tilting in terms of information, knowledge, capacity, opportunity.

A further feature is that with the development of Web.2 and social media there is much greater opportunity for interaction, leading to the impression that we can engage with others and the world 'out there' more readily. Whether this interactivity or connectivity is effective in political terms is a matter to which we will be returning in the next chapter; but in terms of people's behaviour, perception is key. If someone perceives that joining a virtually based group like GetUp! or Avaaz is a more effective way of intervening in the world in terms of their own political interests and concerns, then the knock-on consequences for traditional forms of political participation and organization are considerable.

Adding these elements together gives us a picture of a world in which relatively stable social structures, identities and interests are increasingly under pressure. This is not a uniform or homogeneous process, and social theorists are quick to note the uneven manner in which these processes impact different societies. Texts on the changing composition of contemporary society are full of terms like 'disjuncture' and 'fragmentation', indicating that what goes for one society in one part of the world may not go for another. Nevertheless, there appears to be a degree of consensus not only that fundamental changes are taking place, but also that they are driven by 'globalization', a shorthand for the erosion of the world we were describing in the previous chapter, one with discretely assembled nation states enjoying sovereignty over the affairs taking place within them. As is becoming evident, the nation state is now but one actor at one level of a multi-scalar world. Its citizens look and sound progressively less like each other as the flow of peoples outstrips whatever model of assimilation or integration elites think up to preserve 'the nation'. 'The People' becomes increasingly detached from a sociological reality to describe. The People is being transformed into Everybody, a heterogeneous, increasingly unrepresentable jumble of individuals and identities. As Rosanvallon notes:

The people can no longer be apprehended as a homogeneous mass. It is felt to be rather a series of separate histories, an accumulation of specific situations. Hence societies today increasingly understand themselves in terms of minorities. A minority is no longer merely 'the smaller number'. It has become one of a series of diffracted expressions of the social totality. Society nowadays manifests itself as a long litany of minority conditions. 'People' has become the plural of 'minority'. (Rosanvallon 2011: 4)

Individualization and the erosion of authority

The decline of collective identities and with it the grid or matrix of expectations concerning who belongs where in favour of an 'individualized society' tends to be viewed by much sociological commentary with a mixture of sadness and apprehension. Something is being lost: certainty about who one is, and what one is, where one has come from and where one is going. The result is, according to Bauman, anxiety, alienation, rootlessness (Bauman 2001). We are left 'bowling alone', in Robert Putnam's famous phrase, cast off from the coordinates and relationships that create identity, certainty, a sense of place – all central, so it would seem, to the development of trust in others, in turn a key component in terms of thinking about the basis of representation (Putnam 2000). The danger is that this makes us receptive to various kinds of fundamentalism for those who have lost their bearings, or who need 'crutches', as Agnes Heller puts it, in a world where identity is becoming contingent, uncertain, muddy (Heller 1999: 4–5). And if it doesn't lead to fundamentalism, then there are legions of commentators lined up to say that it leads to narcissistic behaviours: consumerism, the adoption of a materialistic outlook, shallowness, selfishness and a generally self-absorbed attitude. If one were to judge the impact of individualization by a glance at the online edition of the *Daily Mail*, then one might well come away with the impression that politics has succumbed to the mind-numbing consolations of personal 'lifestyle' and the constant admonition to 'look good', 'feel good' and 'enjoy life'. 'Individualization' looks on one reading to be a disaster for the individual. It also looks like a disaster for politics, given that politics concerns the common good and collective life. Bauman is not the only figure who reads individualization as depoliticizing.

These accounts may reflect the tenor of much sociological commentary, indeed much political commentary of both left and right.

Individualization might be read here as 'atomization': the sense of a wrenching of the individual out of the social contexts and communities that created bonds of identity, solidarity, affinity with others. We are left, so it would seem, with a heterogenous mass of individuals – a kind of rootless 'bare life' that serves the needs and interests of elites all too well. However, other readings of modernity emphasize the centrality of what is sometimes referred to as 'reflexivity' to understanding the nature of contemporary subjectivity. The argument here is that the tendency within modernity is to query and question tradition, authority, identity, with the effect that the 'naturalness' of social relations and practices is exposed as socially constructed, and maintained by design. This looks corrosive at one level; but at another it can be read as the basis for opening up social structures and practices to critique, argument, negotiation and reform. All too often, arguments defending authority and tradition mask, so it is argued, the particularistic interests of some against the claims of many others. From this perspective the hypothesis that modernity unsettles congealed practices and traditions and the position of those who guard them is one that might be celebrated, not lamented. It amounts to the adoption of a critical stance as regards inherited traditions and structures that preserve the *status quo*. By extension, *reflexive individualization* implies a self-conscious distancing from collective and aggregate identities, from the idea that one has to be the person or identity that others expect one to be. Easier said than done perhaps, but the direction of travel is clear enough, even for those who lament it. The idea of one's fate as bound up with the destiny of a collective subject, whether it be a class, caste, nation or other identity, is at the very least contested by the idea of the individual as author of his or her own destiny (Heller 1990: 167). Of course, such a notion is replete with difficulty in a world governed by all manner of inequities in terms of access to the resources to operationalize such a notion: access to education, to basic sustenance, to family support, and so forth. Such is the stuff of a range of responses in political theory terms and public policy terms, from theories of global justice, to capability theory, to theories of exploitation and critiques of development. The huge interest in Thomas Piketty's *Capital in the Twenty-First Century* (2014) is witness to the concern with the mismatch between what defenders of capitalism like to claim is the moral basis for markets and the current reality: increasing inequality and lack of access to the means for individual flourishing.

What, then, of the worry articulated by social theorists such as Bauman and Putnam that individualization leads to a loss of authority, or loss of the sense that the individual should feel him- or herself constrained by tradition, received norms, the wisdom of existing institutions and identities? This is certainly a feature of the reflexive account. Indeed reflexivity as it appears in the work of theorists like Gilles Deleuze, Raoul Vaneigem and Agnes Heller can be read as a celebration of the loss of the aura of authority to shape the subject in accordance with dominant needs, interests and ideologies. There is little sense of regret, in other words, that inherited social and political structures might be waning. On the contrary, the rejection of such structures is taken to be the necessary precondition for the re-establishment of social relationships as, at least potentially, something negotiated, dynamic and resting on choices and preferences exercised in the present, as opposed to an inheritance from a real or imagined past. The stakes can therefore be read as a contest between *tradition* and the acceptance of the inherited past as a kind of limit point for ourselves, and *contingency*, or the view that how we live should be determined by ourselves.

The decline of fixed and certain identities, of the inherited expectations that attend membership of a class, ethnicity, nation, may or may not be experienced as loss by any given individual; but it would appear to have important ramifications for the nature of representation and by extension representative politics, which, as noted, has flowed from the availability and acceptance of identities by those being represented. There is no 'working-class politics' if people don't self-identify as working class, if the working class has disappeared or 'died'. Or rather there is, but it is a politics filled with a hollow sound, the politics of *would-be* representatives of the working class finding little echo in their message. And even if aggregate identities have not exactly disappeared, they are certainly under stress. So where does 'individualization' leave representation?

Certain trends and tendencies stand out when it comes to thinking about the impact of individualization on politics. How to summarize these changes?

The crumbling pyramid

Politics under first modernity is a matter of structures and practices built on a 'vertical' basis. As we noted in the previous chapter, politics is framed in terms of the acceptance of hierarchy: the state over society; leaders over led; intellectuals over masses; representatives over the represented. There is an active part and a passive part, a part that possesses power in the interests of the part that does not. The

77

mainstay of hierarchies in terms of political organization is the division of labour, and the ideology that underpinned it: that some people are fitted to do certain tasks and others to undertake lesser ones. Reflexivity would seem to be corrosive of such hierarchies, particularly those based on tradition or received notions of who should be 'in charge'. Under modernity, the idea of the inherited right to lead gives way to other notions based on technical competence, intellectual ability and far-sightedness, wisdom – in turn leading to hierarchies based on notions of desert or merit. But reflexivity is undermining the idea of the 'specialness' of certain categories of individual (*What do you know about it? You're no better than I am*), and this is having an impact in the political field. Negatively, it means that we are less likely than earlier generations to believe in the specialness of politicians and other kinds of representative. Positively, it means that many of the new initiatives and organizations being created by activists and citizens seek quite self-consciously to move away from the model of traditional organizations such as the mass party, trade unions or other large-scale organizations of a kind that we associate with representative politics. New initiatives are, or like to think they are, 'flatter', nimbler. They 'shape-shift' as and when the moment requires it. They are part of an emerging ecology of organizational life based on networks and looser, more contingent arrangements based around distributed power, 'acephalous' or leaderless organizing, greater participation, collaborative work and organizational flexibility.

(Don't) take me to your leader

The decline of hierarchy is increasingly felt in terms of a waning of respect for those in positions of authority. It's an often remarked upon facet of contemporary existence usually reported under shrill headlines concerning the decline in respect for teachers, judges, parents or other authority figures. There's no doubt a lot of truth in the suggestion, and it certainly chimes with a theme we covered earlier in the chapter concerning the fate of politicians at the hands of many electorates around the world. The common denominator is the idea of *positional leadership*, which is the sense that someone occupying a particular position is owed respect on the basis of the position he or she holds, as opposed to the actions he or she performs in it.

As seems to be becoming clearer, positional leadership or authority is under strain. This is not to say that all kinds of leadership or authority are disappearing. But, as is frequently remarked upon in business and management education, we are moving away from the idea that authority and respect flow from the position one holds, to the idea that they are *earned* by virtue of the qualities one displays (Humphrey 2002; Sutton 2010). The ability to connect to others in such fashion has been termed 'emotional intelligence' or EQ – Emotional Quotient (Goleman 2006). Successful leadership is less a question of ordering people around because one is in a position that allows one to do so than it is a matter of generating greater trust through the way in which one comports oneself with employees. Hence the stress in 'leadership training' on integrity, sincerity and a willingness to listen to others, admit mistakes and empathize with those one is seeking to lead.

No doubt much of this is PR for the ideology that underpins today's 'caring capitalism', that of the 'Good Boss', but nonetheless there is a resonance in terms of looking at political leadership. An EQ perspective helps us to read the difference in *style* between exemplary leadership of the kind displayed by leaders such as Gandhi, Havel, Mandela, Walesa, on the one hand, and the leadership of 'politicians', on the other. We seem increasingly to be associating politicians with *positional leadership* as opposed to *exemplary leadership*. As our earlier comments indicated, this was not always the case. The popularity of figures like Churchill and Roosevelt owes much to the fact that they displayed exemplary qualities, qualities which engendered trust, and which motivated people to follow them. The more politicians seem to rely on their *position* to generate authority, the less sense of connection we have to them. They may have a mandate, but, as Rosanvallon notes, this doesn't mean that we *feel* represented by them. Increasingly, having 'a mandate' is becoming divorced from representation, even if it underpins the legitimacy of politicians to govern (Rosanvallon 2011: 214). But governing, and even less ruling, is not the same as representing. This means that politics has an inevitably negative air, a matter of avoiding certain candidates or outcomes more than embracing others; of voting against rather than voting for; of querying, questioning, challenging politicians, as opposed to investing in them for the promise of better times to come. By contrast, exemplary leaders don't need to hold power, and few of them even seek it. Power is often thrust upon them by exigency and by the desire of movements to be led by someone uninterested in power and the benefits and privileges it brings.

The DIY-ification of politics

The collapsing narrative around hierarchy and authority means we are less trusting of others to look after our own interests. The availability of huge amounts of information over the internet means, for example, that many of us check our medical conditions and treatments online instead of relying just on the authority of a doctor. University teachers regularly find themselves being challenged by students who have found some contradictory item or evidence to challenge their pet theories. Lawyers find they are up against individuals who have gained access to relevant statutes or legislation enabling them to defend themselves or to pursue an action. The list goes on. This, too, is what reflexivity looks like: increasing scepticism regarding the 'special' qualities of doctors, professors, lawyers and, of course, politicians.

We are becoming progressively less convinced by the suggestion at the heart of the process of representation, which is that someone else is able to defend my needs or interests better than I am. The idea that intellectuals are better able to understand the path of historical development and thus able to show the masses 'the line of march' belongs to an era where many amongst the working class had little access to sources of knowledge or other means to expand their own horizons, and were often dependent on those with the time to devote to developing an analysis of the present. Intellectuals are no longer privileged in such a fashion. As is often noted, the general standing of intellectuals has declined in the same way as those professionals we have just been discussing (Posner 2009). Today, everyone is an 'expert', or, what amounts to the same, believes him- or herself to be so. What it means in practice is that ordinary citizens have become much less receptive to the idea of politics as an intellectually led undertaking, as opposed to a practice in which everyone's views have equal validity. Intellectual leadership is going the way of positional leadership.

Weber's idea of politics as a 'vocation' described politics as an activity that some may excel at, whilst others do not. It's an idea that is found throughout the history of political thought, and is highly attractive to elites, who have often justified their exalted position in the political division of labour by reference to superior wisdom, intelligence or technical skills. Indeed one of the earliest critiques of democracy came from Plato on precisely the basis that politics was a complex technical matter that required special expertise to manage. As the basis of this notion is eroded, so too is the idea of politics as the preserve of elites, as opposed to an everyday practice that can engage citizens in all manner of ways. Politics is becoming an 'everyday' practice for 'everyday makers', indeed a 'lifestyle' for those who have decided to devote themselves and their time to particular causes (Bang 2004). This poses a challenge to the image of politics as happening in a particular place or setting, and as the preserve of those with a mandate or the authority to represent us. It suggests that politics is everywhere, and that anyone and everyone can be, should be, involved, act, be heard, participate. Politics is becoming an extension of ethics: 'Be the change you wish to see'; GetUp!; 'I am the 1% and I have a voice!'; 'Five things you can do now!' Just as we cannot cede the task of being virtuous to someone else, nor increasingly can we cede the task of confronting injustice, inhumanity, inequality, to someone else. *It's up to us to make a difference.*

Conclusion

What these various changes suggest is that individualization disrupts a certain narrative about the unfolding of democracy and representation. Numerous accounts of the development of democracy note that its chief achievement over the past two centuries has been to evolve in a fashion that brings more citizens, more identities, into political life, by transforming those who previously were not represented into the category of those who are. Slowly, the battle for the vote, for rights, indeed for representation, is being won in the Democratic Revolution (Laclau and Mouffe 1985). Looked at on these terms, democracy has been a great success. The unrepresented are increasingly becoming the represented. Those who were previously excluded are becoming increasingly included. Struggles for recognition continue; and always will – so it seems – as new identities are created and new political demands emerge. Such, for many, is the nature of political contestation under modernity. How, then, to resolve the paradox that at the very moment of its triumph, democracy faces its greatest challenge, not from without, from regimes that are unfriendly to democracy, but from *within*, in the form of a crisis of representation? How can democracy at one and the same time be both the highest form of political development *and* in crisis?

The suggestion here is that globalization, communicative abundance, individualization and the ancillary processes associated with reflexive modernization are disrupting the narrative. The modernizing process has brought into question the validity of the paradigm

81

discussed in the previous chapter. Advances in technology, in the organization of production and in the speed and manner of interactions between peoples and cultures mean that the basis of representation and representative politics is in question. The authority of representatives is becoming harder to maintain. Citizens are becoming more sceptical about the ability of their representatives to provide solutions, demonstrate leadership, guide the nation or the class, or whatever collective identity is held to be pertinent. Increasingly we neither need nor want to be represented by politicians, or would-be politicians. We are moving, remorselessly, away from representation and representative politics towards styles and modes of politics that engage us immediately, directly, *now*. We still have representatives, many of us will still vote, and squabble and argue over what it is that politicians do or don't do in our name. But the aura is gone; the genie is out of the bottle. We are no longer believers in the metanarrative of representation: that our interests are best served if some represent and everyone else is represented. We are becoming *unrepresentable*.

— 4 —

IS THE PARTY OVER?

The rise of representative politics at the turn of the nineteenth century is marked in the emerging democracies of Europe and North America by the onset of contested elections and the creation of political parties. Political parties flourished over the course of the late nineteenth century and into the twentieth, providing a focus for political activity for committed citizens – and even the less committed. They provided a source of solidarity and support for generations of ordinary people, many of whom in turn expended time and energy in their service as activists. Parties became the object of loyalty and affection as they developed deep roots in many communities, as much *social* entities as *political* ones.

In view of the above, it's little surprise to find that the precipitous decline in the membership of political parties in most advanced democracies elicits great soul searching amongst all species of analyst (Dalton 2002; Van Biezen 2004; Whiteley 2011). For political scientists the decline of political parties poses a problem in terms of the legitimating basis of liberal democracy. Conventional political activism takes place in and through political parties. Parties have traditionally been the main source of identification and mobilization of ordinary citizens. They have proved a useful means of *aggregating* or bundling up preferences and interests, in turn giving the impression of representing citizens. In a context where, for example, we see two dominant parties, like the Democrats and Republicans, the pendulum movement between the two aids the sense that parties are integral to the representation of citizens. If it's not 'my time' now, then it will be at some point in the future.

For political theorists, the decline of the party as an organizational *form* is a worry because it suggests that we no longer wish to organize to use the power of the state for the benefit of the deserving or to advance some better vision of how we should live. This offers a diminished vision of democratic contestation, and suggests a descent into technocratic elite-driven governance as opposed to a genuine contest between distinct conceptions of justice or the Good Society (Crouch 2004; Della Porta 2013). On the left, the decline of the party is seen as indicative that politics now longer has the capacity to engage, inspire, move people to action, notwithstanding the impact of neoliberalism, the development of the surveillance state, environmental degradation. We have forsaken the big issues in favour of piecemeal reformist campaigning. Or worse: we have convinced ourselves that tapping away on Facebook or Twitter will displace 'real' political action, that is, action which has lasting effects and social consequences.

The decline of parties is, I think, explicable in terms of the developments we traced in the previous chapter. Politics is undergoing a transformation in terms of citizens' ability and willingness to be represented by others, and particularly by 'politicians'. Politics is becoming individualized, which is often taken to mean that the collective is being sacrificed in favour of personal wants and needs. But that politics is being individualized does not of itself mean that we cannot act *collectively*. It means that we are moving from the collective action of aggregate identities, interests and ideologies to what Michele Micheletti terms 'individualized collective action' (Micheletti 2003), or forms of collective action inspired and carried forward by discrete individuals *acting in common cause*. But if this is not to occur through political parties, how does it work? And if we accept the premise, does this mean that political parties are finished? If so, what are the implications for democracy?

A farewell party?

There are two parts to the story of the evolution of political parties that we need to be attentive to: the *content*, or what it is that parties are for; and the *form*, or what kind of organization political parties are. Some thought is needed concerning each.

Content: what's the matter with the message?

Political parties were set up to represent the needs and interests of various kinds of identities and interests. From the end of the eighteenth century onwards this mission was often framed in terms of *ideologies*. Powerful currents of thought coalesced around certain key ideas concerning human nature, historical development and a social ideal. Some of these currents of thought were highly systematic and based on a particular doctrine, as in the case of communism, which took its cue from the work and leadership of Karl Marx and Friedrich Engels. Others, such as socialism and liberalism, took the form of a more loosely assembled set of ideas, which nonetheless offered a coherent basis for the development of a political programme. Conservatism became a kind of shorthand for an approach modelled on the *anti*-ideological stance of stressing the importance of tradition, continuity and respect for received ways of organizing social and political life. Ideology provided both the impetus for the creation of political parties and their rationale: the attainment of power so as to realize the values or vision embodied in the ideology – usually in the form of a manifesto, programme or platform. Ideologies provide the 'big picture' that makes sense of the world for concerned individuals. Not all parties have a well-developed ideology in the sense of some-thing rooted in a firm doctrine or theoretically mapped account of the world. Some, such as the US parties, have thinner attachments to ideology than those in Europe, Latin America and beyond. But they all try to offer some more or less developed sense of where the ills that confront citizens come from, and how it is that the party will help alleviate them over the long term as well as the short.

As has been discussed over the past half-century, ideology is losing the capacity to connect, inspire and mobilize the populations of the advanced democracies. Different thinkers offer different explana-tions for why this is the case. Daniel Bell suggested that as early as the 1950s ideology had become an irrelevance in societies marked by growing prosperity and a consensus concerning the role of the state in providing certain public goods (Bell 1960). Herbert Marcuse agreed with Bell, but from the opposite end of the political spectrum. He argued that the dominant ideology was so successful at driving out the space for and possibility of critique that politics had become 'one dimensional' or devoid of critical energy (Marcuse 1964). Others, such as Jean-François Lyotard, argue that we have become more scep-tical and pessimistic about politics and therefore less open to the idea that politics offers a path to redemption, liberation or emancipation. Lyotard coined the term 'the postmodern condition' to describe what he called 'an incredulity towards metanarratives' (Lyotard 1984). We no longer believe in the idea of history as the coming to be of a perfected form of society. The world has become too complex, too diverse, for us to imagine that there is a single vision or blueprint that might cure all the ills that confront us. We have become 'pagans' – or non-believers. It's from a similar premise that Ulrich Beck builds his account of the 'Risk Society' (Beck 1992). Politics now concerns the *avoidance of negatives* (crisis and catastrophe), rather than the *building of positives* (emancipation, liberation). The main aim of political action is the preservation of our social and environmental habitat in a world of increasing risk and insecurity.

Underneath the thicket of competing explanations lies a common theme: *the problem of complexity*. Ideologies offer a worldview that supplies answers to the key questions that confront us. At one level ideologies are, as has often been noted, a secular variant of religion. They are a source of truth and hope. They offer the possibility of community, and a structure through which the world can be understood and a future charted, often with the help of charismatic or authoritative figures who help develop or add to that understanding. They simplify the world, offering ready-to-digest analysis combined with prescriptions as to how to improve our lives. Yet whereas religions are thriving, ideologies are declining. Ideologies lack the qualities that have helped religions meet the challenges of individualization. The sense of certainty engendered by religious texts is largely absent, even in doctrinally based ideologies such as communism. It's a point noted by Marxists themselves, a number of whom lament the fact that whereas religion is able to inspire devotion, even fanaticism, communism no longer does. Militancy, in the sense of action inspired by the certainty of truth, is today the preserve of fundamentalists. This is a matter of regret for those like Slavoj Žižek and Alain Badiou who argue that without militancy there can be no radical politics, but just a mushy 'feel good' inclusivity that is afraid to act for fear of upsetting people (Žižek 2002; Badiou 2008). Real politics, muscular politics, needs believers – but the believers are increasingly to be found on the religious right not the left, which has succumbed, so it seems, to postmodernism, identity politics and multiculturalism.

Actions usually speak louder than words, and what has become clear is that whatever appetite there might once have been for 'big vision' politics, politics built on some sense of collective certainty concerning the nature of 'the just' or 'the good' has waned. But we need to be careful before drawing the conclusion that this has dulled the appetite for *politics*. It has certainly dulled the appetite for *ideological politics*, or a politics that is informed and inspired by a clearly articulated vision of how society should look. By contrast, non- or post-ideological forms of politics, and particularly *movement politics*, have exploded. Why?

Movement politics is a form of politics driven less by ideology, however defined, than by a shared sense of *injustice*. One doesn't need a developed account of the ideal society to perceive injustice in colonialism, racial discrimination, child labour, the trafficking of women for the sex industry, the extinction of rare species. Yet injustice has proven to be a powerful spur to action. It is simple and direct. It speaks to values that many share, such as respect, dignity, often formulated in terms of certain rights. It doesn't require an elaborate philosophy or doctrine. It doesn't need spelling out in terms of a comprehensive worldview. It doesn't require ideologues or leaders pointing us in the right direction. Injustice suggests its own solution: the alleviation of an intolerable situation. This is not to say that such interventions are easy to achieve or that they do not require a great deal of organization; they do, as, for example, the decolonizing movements of the twentieth century demonstrate. It wasn't easy to overcome colonial rule, yet movements in India and beyond were able to achieve exactly that by focusing on injustice as the spur to the creation of mass movements. The same is true for the civil rights movement of the 1960s and the 'People Power' movements that brought down communism in Central Europe in the 1980s and 1990s.

The success of social movements is due at least in part to the fact that they are often based on a simple message. Many quite self-consciously avoid 'ideology' or an elaborate doctrine. Ideology, on this reading, divides. It creates believers and non-believers. It creates ideologues, leaders and 'politicians'. The struggle against injustice certainly creates leaders; but they tend to be what we have been terming *exemplary figures* who embody in their actions the simple message they wish to convey. Contrast a Gandhi or a Havel, in other words, with the leaders of political parties. The former seem humble and uninterested in power for its own sake. The latter can seem interested *only* in power.

The decline of ideology has not gone unnoticed by politicians. On the contrary, in recent decades there has been something of a rush to ditch as much ideological 'baggage' as possible in the quest to appeal to the electoral majority. Parties have been busy rebranding themselves the world over in the rush to look *less* committed to an ideology. Examples abound, from the transformation of the British Labour Party into New Labour and the *Partito Comunista Italiano* into *Rifondazione*, to the German Greens. Even the Chinese Communist Party has progressively moderated the language of class war inherited from its Marxist past in favour of an inclusive language with an up-beat message for every strata of society. This is understandable in

87

view of the fact that the rationale of political parties is to seek and retain power. But if they are no longer interested in implementing a distinctive vision, then this leaves citizens wondering what they are for.

Form: what's the matter with the organization?

The traditional political party is built on a functional division of labour, which in turn leads to a particular kind of hierarchy. The rationale of most parties is to seek power for its leadership. The leaders draft the programme. They organize the election and fill the offices of government in the event of electoral success. Other party members occupy a more minor role, whether that be in terms of getting out the vote, distributing pamphlets, raising money, attending party conferences or organizing the catering. In this sense the organization and structure of political parties mirror the traditional model of the division of labour found in organizations under conditions associated with first modernity, where it was clear who gave the orders and who carried them out. It was in its own terms a highly successful formula, and one with which the very many citizens who joined and engaged with political parties found little to contest.

What has become clearer over the past few decades is that many citizens are becoming turned off by styles of politics that raise some up to the role of leaders or 'politicians' whilst others take on lesser roles. This relationship between the leadership and the membership can be more or less dynamic. Party cultures differ. Some are marked by a slow churn of cadres and by the monopolization of leadership positions by members of a particular caste, class, background or ethnicity. Other parties are more dynamic, displaying a high turnover of officials and relatively open processes when it comes to selection and accountability of those entrusted to lead. But the image of the party as a 'vertical' form of practice that gives voice to a select group or elite whilst leaving everyone else undertaking lesser tasks is a factor helping to explain why the politically active might prefer other, more open styles of organizing, and why ordinary citizens are becoming reluctant to engage.

There's a more general point about hierarchies, however, that touches on the changes looked at in the previous chapter. As is well documented in organizational studies, the traditional pyramid model that characterized organizations under first modernity is losing favour. This is signalled by the adoption of a language that contrasts traditional organizational structures to 'flat hierarchies', 'network models', 'self-managing teams', 'delayering', 'distributed power', 'non-leadership'. Much of this, it has to be said, is either aspirational or a form of marketing to make organizations look funky and interesting to clients, and indeed to their own employees. But why would they bother if there hadn't been a shift in terms of how people *perceive* the nature of a successful and engaging organization? Presumably because the old top-down command model looks and feels tired. It speaks to a world that social theorists tell us is in the process of disappearing: a world where people knew their place in the hierarchy and took orders from those who had some superior marking, whether accent, background or education. Life has moved on, and with it the expectations people have about work (Thompson and McHugh 1990; Wilson 2013). Employees increasingly expect to be consulted, to participate and to be 'stakeholders'. They don't expect to be talked down to, instructed, bossed around or given orders by bellowing besuited figures.

In light of these changes, traditional political parties can look outmoded and outflanked by other kinds of 'flatter' or otherwise more involving organizations. The example of the Tea Party in the US is instructive in this respect. The Tea Party owes a great deal of its success not only to its bluntly libertarian message, but also to its *form* (Zernike 2010; Williamson et al. 2011). The Tea Party started out as a loose coalition of those concerned about the direction their government was taking. It quickly snowballed, throwing up leaders who looked and sounded similar to ordinary grassroots activists. Its leaders successfully distanced themselves from the inheritance of 'politicians', giving them the impression that they had stepped out of the grassroots themselves to assume a different kind of leadership position, an exemplary style of leadership, as opposed to the positional leadership of one who rises through the bureaucratic ranks of a large organization. However, once the Tea Party started contesting elections, it began to look and sound less like a network and more like a traditional party. It stumbled into image difficulties. Its apparently folksy leaders began to seem like the politicians they ridiculed as 'distant' and 'out of touch'. Its structures congealed into hierarchies. Much of the initial energy dissipated, leaving its grassroots character looking more like 'astroturf'.

It's not just political parties engaged in electoral politics that have suffered in terms of the loss of members and the general indifference of citizens. Parties of the left, parties with grand ambitions and radical diagnoses, have fared little better. Around the world, communist parties have had to reinvent themselves or risk falling into obsolescence in the wake of a general backlash against the party form on the radical left. Once mighty communist organizations such as the Italian and French Communist Parties endlessly remodel themselves to look less communist, less threatening, and less like they might actually 'change the world'. The UK's Socialist Workers Party (SWP) was so concerned about its self-image that in the wake of the anti-capitalist protests of the early 2000s it set up a front organization, 'Globalise Resistance', to offer an alternative face to the newly mobilized.[1] By contrast with the dowdy class war language of its Trotskyite mother party, Globalise Resistance got down with the language of networks, multitudes and distributed power. To little avail as it turned out. Globalise Resistance was 'outed' as a front organization, and whatever momentum it possessed quickly dissipated into the ether.

Faced with declining memberships, redundant ideologies, the withering of formerly certain identities, which in turn provided the ballast of parties' support, it seems reasonable to conclude that the traditional mass political party is in danger of declining further, perhaps to irrelevance in certain contexts. However, there is no immediate or foreseeable prospect of political parties dying out. Many representative democracies are structured in such a way as to make it highly unlikely, if not inconceivable, that we will see the end of political parties. Some electoral systems feature 'party lists' that make it difficult, if not impossible, for independent candidates to feature (Lawson 2010). Others deploy 'first past the post' electoral systems, making it more remote that independent or minority candidates can win. Even where systems *are* constructed to permit the emergence of independent or 'non-party' candidates, they still require a party-like machine to get organized for competing at an election. They need to collect signatures, print materials and brochures, develop a website, raise funds, connect with the media, write speeches, and so forth. All this requires organization. Whether such an organization is called a party or a 'coalition' or 'bloc' or whatever amounts to the same thing: if you want political power, then you need to stand for election, and if you want to stand for election, you need a party, or a party-like organization.

So what, then, is the fate of the mass parties? Decline, so it would seem, to the point where they become withered imitations of the once great organizations they used to be. What is left, as political commentators often note, are post-ideological 'brands' with vague connotations that help them to differentiate themselves from other offerings in the political supermarket. As for any brand seeking market share, they are full of promises of 'a new beginning', 'real change', 'change you can believe in', in much the same way that washing powders are continually remarketed with 'a new and improved' formula. The less firm, less fixed on a specific ideological project or identity, the more a political party can reinvent itself to appeal to the possible constituency and thereby increase its attractiveness. Political parties are now much less the bearers of distinct visions than vehicles for rival leadership groups seeking power. This is implied in what political commentators call 'the presidentialization of politics' (Poguntke and Webb 2007). If politics is no longer about ideology or substantively different programmes, then it becomes a matter of the different leadership qualities and traits of would-be presidents and prime ministers. Do we like the neatly suited toothy figure in the red corner, or the neatly suited toothy figure in the blue corner?

Politics after and beyond the party

As we shall see, the party is by no means over. There can be no over for the party as long as democracy remains a representative, and indeed party-based, form of governance. However, political commentators are a little hasty if they think that the cause of the decline of the traditional political party lies exclusively or even primarily with the generalization of feelings of apathy amongst citizens. Politics is alive and well, as we have had occasion to remark; it's just changing in character, and in particular becoming *individualized*. Whether political parties will be able to prove attractive to citizens is thus increasingly a story about how parties will adapt to these trends. But before addressing the matter directly, we need to unpack the key characteristics of individualization in terms of how citizens mobilize. Thinking about what we have already covered, key elements include the following:

The shift from mediated forms of political action to immediate forms of action. Representative politics is what might be termed *mediated* politics. It's a politics where someone else speaks and acts on one's behalf. It can therefore seem a relatively passive politics in the sense that representative politics embraces a distinction between those who lead and those who follow, or take on more minor roles. In practice the distinction may not be as marked as these labels suggest. Historically, many citizens were attracted to political parties because they wanted to make a difference, they wanted to *act*, rather than be passive spectators. The term 'activist' used, therefore, to be strongly associated with work in and for a party. Not any longer. Increasingly, 'activist' refers to those working *outside* political parties in 'disaffiliated' contexts. 'Party politics' has, it seems, become a turn-off for those who want to act, contest, resist, engage. Now they seek more *immediate* forms of activism, other ways and means in which they can act, *as opposed to* mandating someone else to act or speak in their name.

It's at least in part the desire to act that lies behind the upsurge of initiatives such as protests, demonstrations, carnivals, sit-ins and occupations. One of the appeals of direct action lies in the sense that one is doing something, directly, *now*. There is in these forms of activism a strong sense of engagement and participation, more so, it would seem, than in party-based activism. There are also more risks involved, which may heighten the sense that one is a participant and actor rather than a spectator. This is not to say that one wishes to act alone, or without the support and help of others. 'Individualized collective action' is still *collective* action, even though it takes the form of individuals using their power as, for example, consumers to campaign against sweatshops, improve the pay of workers or shame corporations into improving the conditions for those employed off shore (Micheletti 2003).

A further impetus to direct action is the fact that the *repertoires for acting* have expanded enormously in recent decades. One of the areas of significant growth has been hacktivism, or cyber protest (Pickerill 2003; van de Donk et al. 2005). One of the most prominent activist networks in the world, Anonymous, whose adoption of the Guy Fawkes mask became a worldwide symbol of protest, is virtually based. With corporations and public authorities now highly dependent on the maintenance of networks and electronic communication, opportunities abound for activists to disrupt their work through a broad repertoire of interventions, from hacking and pinging (i.e. swamping servers through automated message bounce-back), to the disabling of whole networks. Much of this activism is in the form of individuals working on a specific action or initiative which when multiplied with the work of others can impact the activity of institutions or governments against which they have an animus.

The shift from doctrinal or ideological politics to a politics of contestation. As we noted above, the decline of ideology is a key feature of the contemporary political landscape. But this doesn't necessarily equate to apathy or indifference, as is often supposed. Part of the story of decline is the rejection of ideology and ideologists in favour of a different, anti- or non-ideological stance, often with the aim of encouraging the individual to assume ethical and moral responsibility for his or her own actions instead of submitting to imperatives from a party leadership. More generally, the decline of ideologically based activisms has been accompanied by the rise of activisms with the objective of *contesting injustice*. Some injustices can be very specific and concrete, as, for example, in the case of a particular development, a particular policy or the condition of a particular group or species. Sometimes they can be much more general. The emergence of the anti-globalization movement and large-scale protests against the World Trade Organization and the G8 in the late 1990s and 2000s were triggered by the sentiment that neoliberalism should be contested. Whilst the slogan of the Global Justice Movement, 'Another world is possible!', suggested an ideological solution, the practices of the movement as embodied in initiatives such as the World Social Forum and the convergence centres that accompanied many protests and demonstrations were designed to promote dialogue and the free play of ideas and perspectives, much to the irritation, as we have noted, of those who felt it needed to generate a singularity of vision and purpose to be effective. Initiatives such as these are less concerned with establishing a new kind of sovereign power, a new normative vision, than with generating what John Holloway terms 'anti-power', or a stance of refusal or resistance that in turn sustains 'autonomous', disaffiliated or de-centred forms of organization and relations (Holloway 2002).

There is a significant difference between ideological politics with a firm sense of development towards an ideal or normatively better vision of society and a politics that contests various aspects of the present. This indicates a shift from a state-centric view of power to the idea of 'everyday' resistances, tactics, networks, that recuperate power in order to address injustices immediately and directly (Day 2004). An injustice can be attacked in a variety of different ways, using a variety of tactics. We mentioned above the example of the campaign against sweatshops, which was the focus for a great deal of activism in the early 2000s. But the desire to combat sweatshops doesn't dictate the particular way in which activists address that issue. Some believe the best way of affecting the behaviour of corporations is to use their own power as consumers. Others have taken it upon themselves to organize a sit-in or a protest at the company headquarters. Others lobby politicians or representatives directly. The point is that there are many different ways in which individuals can draw attention to an injustice and seek to overcome it. How individuals

93

adapt and use their time and energy is not dictated from elsewhere. They are not tied to a formal organization, unless they want to be. It's this element of flexibility combined with responsibility that is a key hallmark of contemporary styles of activism, but the flexibility and responsibility come from the fact that the activism itself is quite different in nature and form to the activisms of the party. It is 'disorganized', in the sense of being highly contingent, with the group or collective avoiding those practices that lead to the development of an organization of a bureaucratic kind promoting or 'representing' the permanent interests of some group or identity (Robinson and Tormey 2005; Gautney 2012).

The shift from hierarchical forms of organization to looser, flatter forms of organizing such as alliances, coalitions, networks, affinity groups and forms of 'non-organizing': 'auto-organizing', swarms, crowds. The explosion of activisms orientated towards addressing injustices has led to a proliferation of different kinds of organization, from affinity groups, blocs, coalitions and platforms, to direct action groupings, networks and virtual hubs of online activists. Many contemporary groupings style themselves as 'horizontal' as opposed to the more 'vertical' style of organization that we find in political parties. Horizontal organizations see themselves as above all participatory and collaborative. This is often at the cost of slower and more deliberative styles of decision-making orientated to the creation of consensus, as opposed to the 'majoritarian' tendency latent in representative forms of politics, where voting is the norm and a 'winner takes all' ethic reigns.

In recent protests, occupations have often been accompanied by the creation of assemblies or other deliberative forums to encourage wide participation and engagement, the rotation of key roles such as Chair or Speaker, the creation of sub-committees to promote involvement and facilitate self-organization. However, that such styles of organization aim at consensus and active participation doesn't mean that this is always what results. Horizontal initiatives and groupings have long been criticized for tolerating *informal* hierarchies, for example of male activists as opposed to female ones, or older, more articulate individuals over younger and less experienced ones, or white, middle-class speakers over minority and working-class participants (Alcoff 1991; Freeman 2013). Simply styling a grouping or organization as 'non-party' or 'horizontal' does not, in other words, equate to the realization of an inclusive and participatory politics; and often they fall someway short of the ideal. Nonetheless, there is a hunger evident

94

in the success of contemporary initiatives to at least seek a more engaging and involving style of politics, a politics that is participatory as opposed to representative; collaborative as opposed to directive; democratic as opposed to hierarchical.

With the emergence of ICT and social media, other styles and forms of interaction are becoming more prevalent, notably 'swarm'- or 'crowd'-based groupings. The concept of the swarm is intended to convey a sense of collective intelligence of a de-centred, leaderless or 'dis-organised' kind (Arquilla and Ronfeldt 2000; Miller 2010). The idea is that a shared sense of opportunity or threat provokes a strong reaction amongst a group of people who share similar aims and goals. This emergent propensity for otherwise loosely affiliated individuals to combine relatively spontaneously is one of the most remarked upon aspects of contemporary politics (Shirkey 2009; Castells 2012; Mason 2012). Such faith in the self-constituting properties of collective action is probably a little overblown. To paraphrase Cornelius Castoriadis, 'Spontaneity requires a lot of organization.' He was writing in the context of the left's eternal debate on the virtues of the Leninist party, which has always been held up by its supporters as the acme of working-class organization. What he meant was that spontaneity was still something that had to be created and planned for by activists. Political action does not occur 'out of nothing'. It's a fair point. Even today's 'spontaneous' actions, such as 15M (see Chapter 5), are the result of activists organizing an event, in this case the activists of ¡Democracia Real YA! (DRY) working together to plan the occupation of towns and squares. On the other hand, no one led the uprising of the *Indignados*, the Arab Spring or Occupy in the same way that Lenin led the Bolsheviks or Mussolini the Italian Fascists, underpinned by a vertically organized party structure, full-time officials and a standing bureaucracy. Instead, individuals who shared common cause combine to create initiatives and protests, some enduring, others less so.

Attention to the very many different ways in which citizens can act offers a rather different impression to that we sometimes get from political commentators lamenting the decline of political engagement. Whilst it remains true that at least part of the story of the withdrawal from representative politics is the growing apathy and disinterest of ordinary citizens, there's a lot more to the story than this. The emergence of individualized, immediate, autonomous, non-representative styles of politics associated with demonstrations, protests, social movements, lobbying and the creation of myriad groups and organizations devoted to combating injustice gives witness to another facet of the current conjuncture. This is the emergence of 'counter-' or 'negative' democratic tendencies – of anti-power and anti-politics (Rosanvallon 2008). This style of politics is much less predictable, and harder to track, which is one reason why it can fly under the radar. In addition it is often event-based, with bouts of activity followed by lulls and silences, giving the impression that there is little going on and that apathy reigns. In reality it might be more accurate to describe the absence of activity as a 'pause' in an on-going cycle of episodic activism, protest, resistance. The capacity of citizens to organize and interact outside and beyond the mainstream, beyond political parties and electoral organizations, was always challenging. By the end of the 1990s, however, at least some of the barriers to organizing were about to be removed.

Social media: the quantum leap forward?

No doubt for some reading this book it will be a surprise to have got this far without touching directly on the impact of ICT and social media, particularly given the much-discussed role of the latter in politics 'kicking off' around the world in the wake of the Arab Spring (Brooke 2012; Castells 2012; Mason 2012; Hill 2013). This should not be read as implying scepticism on my part about the importance of social media in the development of new political forms and initiatives, though there *are* plenty who doubt the value of social media in terms of developing the capacity of ordinary people to change matters for the better (Dean 2009; Gladwell 2010; Morozov 2012). As Jodi Dean argues, 'Valued as the key to political inclusion and democratic participation, new media technologies strengthen the hold of neoliberalism and the privilege of the top 1% of people on the planet' (Dean 2009: 47–8; see also Morozov 2012).

Nevertheless, social media are a game changer as far as the development of *forms and styles* of horizontal organizing are concerned. The emergence of new social media is not the *cause* of the proliferation of new repertoires of activism. Nor is it to blame for the decline of the political party. As I have been arguing, this is located in the larger changes we have been discussing in terms of the development of modern societies. Rather, social media are a *catalyst* for the individualization of politics, undercutting the rationale of representative bodies and practices and bringing forward new styles of politics. How?

Social media make it easier and faster to generate and disseminate images, film, commentary, information, blogs. A key aspect of social media is that they challenge the ability of elites and authorities to control the flow of information. The advent of the smartphone with a built-in camera and social networking means that images and messages can be relayed in real time, disrupting the ability of authorities to control coverage of protests, demonstrations, abuses of human rights, police or army brutality, and suchlike. Over and again this facility to generate content has provided a spark to the escalation of efforts to resist or overturn authoritarian practices and regimes, whether it be demonstrations by peasants in China against land evictions, young Iranians seeking greater personal freedom or citizens protesting against the corruption of politicians in Tunisia.

The circulation of images, the generation of memes and hashtags with a subversive intent, create a climate of scepticism and critique, of 'everyday' resistance, which in the right circumstances can lead to further actions and initiatives with a view to indirectly or directly challenging authorities. The phrase 'knowledge is power' may be a cliché, but it's a cliché for a reason. Perhaps the most powerful weapon in the hands of the authorities is the ability to control what it is that ordinary people come to understand as the world around them, and how they do so. In previous generations, authoritarian regimes took stringent measures to control the flow of information, going as far in the case of the old Communist Bloc of controlling the use of photocopiers and typewriters and otherwise making it very difficult to reproduce text and images. The result was that information of a seditious kind appeared as 'samizdat', which is to say, underground copy, passed from hand to hand and person to person. Given that popular uprisings against authoritarian regimes are typically the result of *momentum*, or large numbers of people acting quickly, it is easy to see why this tactic of controlling information was and is still regarded as key to staving off serious threats to authority.

Social media make it easier to find those with whom one has an affinity or who share common cause. Before the internet it might have taken considerable effort to find those who shared one's political beliefs or those with whom one could make common cause. And the more arcane, esoteric, risky or marginal one's interests, the harder it became. Without an already existing network of people in the know with whom one could consult and share experiences, one might feel that it was just not worth following up. The internet changes all this. A quick Google search will reveal organizations, initiatives, groups, individuals, who share one's interests, whether that be the freeing of Tibet, the saving of the African penguin or the promotion of children's rights in Rwanda. Many of these causes have Facebook pages, Twitter accounts or other means by which one can interact to find out more.

Social media mean one is never alone in one's anger, disgust or desire to act and initiate something. They break down the barriers that once existed towards the creation of groups: geography, distance, time, resources. The barriers to interacting with others who share one's beliefs, values and opinions are now so low as to be almost negligible. Where once it took a great deal of energy and perhaps courage to find others with the same convictions, now the reverse is true. It is *so* easy to find others that the problem is selecting which amongst the many groups, individuals and organizations to choose from to interact with. This facility to engage others has other effects. It can feed *pickiness*. Where once my concern to save the African penguin might have led to my joining the Green Party or an environmental action group, the ability to find others who share my exact concern with the African penguin means that I can concentrate on working with others on this very particular issue. If that approach is replicated, then that can imply a fragmentation and morsellation of political energies. But it need not. As recent events such as the Arab Spring illustrate, there are centripetal as well as centrifugal potentials in social media. Just as they make it easier for those with very discrete or particular interests to find each other, so the obverse is equally true: those with a vague or undefined animus against a given regime or political figure can be mobilized more easily and quickly than was previously the case.

Social media make it easier to organize groups. Just as it is easy to find others who share one's opinions or convictions, now it is much easier to create groups. Groups were once difficult to create. They needed a lot of effort. Political parties were at one level the obvious response of those who wanted to create permanency for a group. How else was one to hold those together with similar values than to create some sort of standing body that would take upon itself the task of communicating to others, bringing them together and mobilizing them? Social media have made this function, if not redundant, then a lot more straightforward. There are now few costs in maintaining a group. This doesn't mean to say that the kind of groups created by social media have the same qualities as political parties. Because it is so easy to create a group, the emotional investment in maintaining a group can be shallow. To choose the 'like' button on a Facebook page is very little commitment compared to that associated with membership of a political party. In researching the previous chapter, I joined GetUp! and Avaaz, a minor matter of sending in my email address and confirming my interest. No fee. No obligations in terms of time and resources. I'm now a member of these organizations, but if every member mimics my current level of involvement, they will fade as quickly as they emerged. Groups created using new technologies can be fleeting, temporary, here today and gone tomorrow. It doesn't mean they *have* to be like this, but the cost of the creation of a group is directly reflected in the changed habits and expectations of group membership. Since it costs so little to join a group, there is little to be lost leaving a group the moment one feels it appropriate to do so. The ecology of groups created through social media is now quite different to what it was before. Groups can spring up overnight and can disappear just as quickly.

Social media make it easier to initiate events and actions. Where once it was a major feat of logistics as well as dangerous to organize a protest or a demonstration, this, too, has become easy, if not without risk. As we have repeatedly seen since 2011, a suggestive tweet, an image of police brutality or an anonymous Facebook page with an idea for a protest or an action can lead to hundreds or thousands of people taking to the streets or joining an action. Of course the conditions need to be ripe. Activists have had to become sophisticated in terms of gauging whether any particular initiative or action is likely to be successful or not based on the speed of the uptake on the relevant Facebook page or Twitter account. Social media thus act as a relay and barometer. A rapid take-up of an initiative demonstrates the strength of feeling about a particular issue, in turn relayed back to activists seeking a mobilization. A slow take-up indicates waning or marginal interest, which may in turn lead to activists calling an initiative off or suggesting a different course of action. This is also symptomatic of a novel mode of leadership compared to that associated with the traditional political party or social movement. Leaders in the virtual environment are those who are able to read the mood on the streets, to suggest appropriate initiatives and actions and relay that to other activists using inventive or eye-catching virtual tags that will then hopefully resonate and create a sense of momentum and desire to be involved. An early example of crowd or swarm activism was UK Uncut, created in 2010 to contest the new Cameron Government's austerity agenda and to 'out' large corporations based in the UK who used off-shore arrangements and tax loopholes to minimize their tax liability. Originally conceived by a handful of activists, the initiative used social media to suggest flash sit-ins and occupations, leading to a rapid take-up with hundreds and occasionally thousands of ordinary citizens turning up to take part in protests. On one occasion a 15-year-old secondary school pupil put out a call to blockade a local Vodafone store and was amazed to find a large crowd gathered outside readying for an occupation.[2]

To use James Scott's phrase, social media are becoming an important new 'weapon of the weak' (Scott 1987). They greatly enhance the capacity of ordinary people to organize, protest and otherwise make their feelings known to elites. Yet what is becoming clearer is that this is not a one-way street. The revelations of Edward Snowden regarding the activities of the US National Security Agency are sobering for anyone interested in the politics of social media. The US and its immediate allies have been gathering 'metadata' of all kinds, and in particular data from social media, to create the basis for the detailed mapping of the interactions of every adult in the advanced democracies, and probably everywhere else as well.[3] In effect every person who has ever used Facebook, Google or Twitter has left behind an indelible track of connections and associations of huge use to intelligence agencies. Will this insight mean that the use of social media will become off limits to those seeking to develop mobilizations in contentious contexts or around contentious issues? Possibly; but the less people feel they have to lose, the more likely they are to disregard the thought that they are being watched. As is becoming more apparent, many of today's mobilizations are born of a sense of increasing desperation around issues such as the cost of living, evictions, austerity measures, the behaviour of corrupt elites, the hiving off of natural resources, environmental degradation. The angrier and more desperate people become, the less the Benthamite strategy of total surveillance is likely to impact their actions.

Mobilization after social media: from representation to resonance

Whatever the threat exposed by the Snowden revelations, it is clear that social media are transforming the ecology of politics in a dramatic way. The key changes are these:

From slow train to evanescence. Politics used to have an architectural dimension to it. It was about building: building a party, building support, building a programme. Building used to take time, effort,

100

resources. It's partly for this reason that representation seems such a natural mode of doing politics to so many. Politics required a division of labour because organizing and building take time. Social media have changed this. It is now no longer laborious to build groups, parties, initiatives, protests, actions. Because it is much easier, groups, organizations, networks, come and go, ebb and flow, in a new evanescent ecology. What is true for groups goes increasingly for new political parties as well. The new parties are no longer substantial organizations, but vehicles of convenience. They can be 'one-hit wonders', contesting a single election perhaps even in a single constituency, only to disappear as fast as they were created. In the 2013 Australian general election, fifty-four political parties contested seats, including the Australian Sports Party, the Motoring Enthusiasts Party, the Coke in the Bubblers Party (meaning 'Free Coca-Cola for everyone') and the gnomically titled Future Party. In Spain over four hundred parties have been created since 2010. Parties are proliferating. Why? Largely because social media have made it so much easier, less time consuming and less expensive to create them. Herein lies an important coda to the preceding discussion. Evanescence does not eliminate the need for or the possibility of political parties. Rather, the political party can itself be the vehicle for an evanescent, immediate, suggestive politics – here today and, equally, gone tomorrow. Political parties have, as it were, joined the party.

From Big Brother to V is for Vendetta. As is becoming increasingly apparent, social media are changing the nature of the relationship between citizens and the state. This is having a dramatic effect on our perception of the relationship between politicians and people. Politics is something that used to take place somewhere else. Politics happened in and around elections, after which politicians get on with governing and citizens went back to their private lives and concerns. With the ease of mobilizing, this image is changing, and it is changing in ways that are perhaps even more pertinent in non- or partially democratic settings than in democratic ones. Mobilizations in Egypt, Turkey, Bulgaria, Brazil, Thailand and Hong Kong have shown that social media provide the basis for spontaneous and acephalous or 'headless' organizing. As we noted above, social media feed off what we might term suggestibility. Generalized feelings of resentment can very quickly translate into significant mobilization on the streets with a few trigger hashtags, and someone taking the lead in suggesting an initiative or an event. Relatively minor complaints such as a rise in the price of public transport or an inappropriate development can trigger an outpouring of anger and disillusionment, leading to mass mobilizations and the paralysis of public life for days and weeks, as in Brazil and Turkey since 2013. Where once politicians looked forward to the period between elections as one of relative peace and calm, increasingly such periods are punctuated by mobilizations, the presentation of new demands and an atmosphere of quasi-insurgency, putting them on the back foot. The discussion of Snowden shows that there are still risks even in spontaneous mobilizing. However, this is unlikely to deflect the over-arching tendency, which is for social media to shape the nature and manner of interactions to an increasing degree.

From representation to resonance. Social media are accelerating the decline of the paradigm of representation in favour of a paradigm of *resonance*. Political parties, leaders, organizations, used to seek members, followers, believers, whom in turn they could represent. And they could represent 'them' in an active/passive relationship because the ability of the singular voice to be heard was so difficult that it was easy for politicians to speak and act on behalf of others without fear that those 'others' would somehow find their own voice. Now that the others can combine much more easily, the relationship is breaking down, and with it the nature of the practices and expectations that underpinned mobilization. The perception, increasingly, is that citizens don't need representatives and politicians to make themselves heard or to act. They can do it for themselves in the expectation that others will want to join in or support their efforts, perhaps in a modest gesture such as a 'like' on a Facebook page, but perhaps also in something more substantial, such as joining a sit-in, an occupation or the creation of a new assembly. New parties will come and go. Some will resonate and be relatively successful; others will cause a momentary flicker before disappearing. The point is that the new political ecology is creating a different *kind* of political party, parties that are better adapted to a politics of speed, velocity, resonance – as opposed to the slow, careful, patient 'representative politics' that created the traditional mass political party. These are pop-up parties, single-issue parties, even 'private parties' like billionaire mine magnate Clive Palmer's Palmer United Party. Here today, gone tomorrow.

Conclusion

What's happening to politics, to mobilization? What is becoming evident is that the ecology that sustained the primacy of the political party is changing dramatically. That ecology was based upon a certain image in relation to sovereignty and state. With the waning of the idea of the sovereign as able to represent a unified and singular people, political parties emerged to permit and encourage a freer flow of opinions and ideas. This worked as long as individuals recognized themselves in terms of the identities and interests associated with the main political parties. But these collective identities and interests are under great stress owing to the larger changes taking place in contemporary society. Traditional parties find themselves mimicking each other, and generating the sense that there is little now to choose between them. The style and form associated with mobilization via the political party have become progressively outmoded by comparison with other kinds of mobilization principally associated with social movements and the event-based activism of protests and demonstrations.

Social media have accelerated the tendency by making it much easier for activists to organize independently of the mainstream. They have generated the sense that politics can be an activity engaging citizens directly and immediately as participants rather than as those who need to be or who want to be represented. In short the new repertoires of organizing groups and events are both *fed by* and *feed upon* the individualization of politics: its transformation into a field of direct engagement as opposed to representation. But as recent events illustrate, the evolution of this new participatory dynamic poses threats as well as opportunities for the institutions and practices of representative democracy. At one level it might offer the impression of greater citizen engagement – 'critical citizens' taking it upon themselves to supplement the normal business of politics through actions such as lobbying and petitioning. This aids the image of representative democracy as a capacious form of politics able to respond to the needs and interests of citizens in various ways. However, there is another dynamic at work, a dynamic that undermines or queries representation and representative politics.

As is becoming evident, the removal of barriers to organizing, deliberating, participating, sets in motion a practice that, at least implicitly, queries the rationale of representation, of that disjunctive logic we described in Chapter 2. Why do we need representatives when it is so easy (so it seems) to have a voice, to participate, to engage with others? Why do we need leaders, politicians, representatives? The result can be an almost *insurrectional* dynamic producing a sense of siege, as public squares and spaces are occupied and become the location for all manner of participatory experiments, carnivals and displays of solidarity, autonomy, defiance, rebellion. This is not 'participation', or 'joining in', so much as querying, contesting and opting out. Sheldon Wolin labels this emergent political logic 'fugitive democracy', implying a kind of withdrawal from the processes that legitimate the present system (Wolin 1996). Michael Hardt and Antonio Negri deploy terms such as 'exodus' and 'exile' similarly to imply a collective disengagement from representative institutions and practices, and the setting in motion of initiatives that undermine or 'refuse' representation (Hardt and Negri 2009). Representative democracy seems capacious enough to accommodate those who do not want or need to be represented. But is it capacious enough to accommodate those who challenge its very logic, who occupy its public spaces, who refuse representation? Can we envisage a democracy of the unrepresentable?

— 5 —

CITIZENS AGAINST REPRESENTATION

So far our discussion has been held at a high level of generality. We have been trying to trace the long-term trends and tendencies affecting representative politics. There's nothing wrong with a high level of generality *per se*, but unless it has some anchor in what is happening on the ground, there's a danger of a disconnect between theory and practice, and of generating an analysis that obfuscates more than it illuminates. I have provided examples as we have been going along of the kind of politics and the kind of initiatives that signal how the crisis is playing out, the new forms of activism and the discourse that underpins it. But it will be useful to pause the over-arching narrative to look at a case study that illustrates in greater detail some of the changes we have been discussing.

The case is the on-going mobilizations that have been taking place in Spain since 2011. This is associated with the emergence of the *Indignados* ('the angry'), a term used by citizens to describe themselves in relation to the events of 15 May 2011, or '15M', as they became known. These events were triggered by those of the Arab Spring and in particular the occupation of Tahrir Square, which was a gesture of frustration with political elites and the state of democracy in Egypt. The gesture resonated in Spain, enough to inspire similar occupations in virtually every city and town across the country. This in turn was a trigger for Occupy Wall Street and the very many other initiatives carrying the 'Occupy' name that quickly proliferated across the world.

Why is this a good case study? Spain is a mature democracy with a stable political system that has not suffered debilitating crises or shocks since the adoption of a democratic constitution in 1975 (Heywood and Grugel 1995). It is a relatively wealthy country with

105

a good standard of living and high levels of political literacy. Whilst political extremism is not unknown in contemporary Spain, its politics is conventionally liberal-democratic. General elections are characterized by the pendulum shift familiar in European politics from centre right (*Partido Popular* – PP) to centre left (*Partido Socialista Obrero Español* – PSOE) and back again. Spain is in most respects an exemplary representative democracy, one widely regarded as a 'good citizen' in terms of its engagement in the region and beyond. The emergence of the *Indignados* is significant from the point of view of the questions that concern us. Here is a mass mobilization of an apparently novel kind. It embraces many different elements of Spanish society sparked by the widely shared perception that the democratic system has run aground. The story of the *Indignados* is one being repeated around the world as citizens organize against austerity, corruption, the deafness of elites, recession, dispossession and myriad other causes. Examining the Spanish mobilizations should therefore offer us some further clues about the nature of the politics we are witnessing and where it is heading.[1]

The Spanish crucible

Some context will be useful. After the Franco dictatorship finally came to an end in 1975, Spain quickly established itself as a stable democracy with relatively high levels of growth for the next three decades. A lot of this growth was speculative in character and focused on property development. Ordinary Spaniards were strongly encouraged by the government to take out mortgages even when they were unlikely to pay them back. The rate of building exploded notwithstanding high rates of interest (Charnock et al. 2011).

When the GFC hit in 2008, many developers were caught out and went bankrupt within months. Unemployment, already high by European standards, surged. Regional governments, which had borrowed heavily on the national as well as international markets, struggled to repay their debts, leading to a crisis in regional as well as state finances. Public sector employment was cut, along with spending and investment in health, education and social services. Very soon Spain was subject to supervision by the so-called Troika (the European Commission, the International Monetary Fund, the European Central Bank), which had taken upon itself the task of ensuring that national governments in the EU were implementing austerity measures leading to the reduction of public debt.

Economic crisis was quickly conjoined by political crisis over the course of 2010–11. What became apparent as the media probed the causes of the economic breakdown was the complicity of the political class in the crisis. Many politicians were implicated in corruption and forms of clientelism and croneyism. Even members of the Spanish royal family, hitherto presented by the media as a bulwark of stability in the period after the transition, were fingered by the media.[2] The crisis was endemic. It seemed that politicians of all parties and political persuasions were involved, and at all levels of government. Political breakdown did not seem very far away, with perhaps worse to come: a state of emergency, perhaps even a military intervention of the kind not unfamiliar in Spain's recent past.

With the crisis deepening in Spain in early 2011, calls to occupy squares spread across social media, led by media-savvy activists from the collective *¡Democracia Real YA!* using Twitter and Facebook (Andronikidou and Kovras 2012). The proliferation of hashtag slogans associated with 15M encapsulated some of the flavour of protest: #spanishrevolution, #globalrevolution, #15mani, #sinmiedo, #acampadasol, #nonosvamos, #yeswecamp (Postill 2013). This led to a 'callout' for occupation of public squares on 15 May 2011. On the day itself millions took to the streets, with occupations taking place in public squares in over fifty cities and towns. One authoritative source puts the number taking part as between 6.5 and 8 million citizens (FnfEurope 2013). In a pattern to be repeated, assemblies were held to discuss the nature of the crisis, allocate tasks in relation to organizing the occupations and keep people informed about the reaction of the authorities (Castañeda 2012; Fuster Morell 2012). Debates and discussions were held, music and art featured, promoting a sense of carnival as well as protest. Many of the occupations lasted for weeks, with assemblies being held regularly even when an occupation had ceased.

The months following 15M were marked by a stand-off between political elites and grassroots movements. The former were able to cling on to power without resort to emergency measures of the kind familiar in the history of endemic crises such as this. The role of the EU and other international bodies such as the IMF were crucial in shoring up the Spanish state and banks with bailouts. Crisis had been averted on the basis that Spain was too big to fail – or to be allowed to fail by powerful supranational bodies, including the EU. Spain would not suffer the kind of devastating crisis that creates a political vacuum and instability. On the other hand, Spanish politics appeared stagnant, devoid of life or power to determine outcomes for itself.

107

Power seemed elsewhere, perhaps amidst the combination of national bodies, supranational institutions and the corporations whose threats to disinvest were a source of consternation in an environment of already high unemployment and fears about the future of the young. Spain had become a 'zombie democracy' (Giroux 2011). Whatever motion could be detected was the result of promptings from outside Spain itself: the need of supranational bodies for a system of governance that could be trusted to maintain law and order, the paying back of debts and the framework that enabled key industries and corporations to function.

15M as event

Even on the basis of the minimal information offered above, certain elements stand out in terms of the overall story of the transformation of politics and mobilization described in the previous chapter:

The centrality of ICT and social media. 15M has already become a key reference point in understanding the impact of social media in terms of mobilization and organization (Hughes 2011; Castells 2012; Mason 2012). Citizens angered by the actions of the government in response to austerity measures sent out hashtags amongst their own networks that quickly caught the attention of other citizens and activists, spawning further slogans and suggestions for action (Toret 2013). Such was the volume of exchanges that the suggestion to occupy Spain's public spaces resonated, was repeated and was reaffirmed in hundreds of thousands of individual actions. On the day itself, as we have seen, citizens took it upon themselves to occupy, demonstrate, remonstrate, across fifty or so town and cities. There's nothing new about protests and demonstrations; far from it. What *is* new is the *speed* with which they can come about, spread and take on significance in social and political terms. What we are learning is that individuals can find common cause in ways that were virtually unthinkable a decade ago.

A mobilization of the unrepresentable. The emergence of the term *Indignados* to describe those engaged in the protests is noteworthy. The exact provenance of the term is uncertain, but the most obvious point of reference is Stéphane Hessel's pamphlet *Indignez-vous!* (literally 'Get Angry!'), originally published in 2009, and reportedly selling over a million copies in Spain alone (Hessel 2011). The term

Indignados is self-identifying. Anyone can join in on whatever basis they see fit, and read whatever purpose they have in mind into the protests and occupations themselves. This was not the mobilization of a pre-existing or established identity ('the working class', 'the People'), but that of the angry and discontented embracing those who might otherwise share little in common. It was a mobilization of those who wanted to *find* something in common – individually and collectively – without the help of others to tell them what they should be doing or how they should be doing it, without intellectuals, representatives, those who could show them 'the line of march'.

The primacy of participation and the assembly form. As quickly became apparent, the institutional forms, practices and processes of the occupations were participatory and dialogical, which is to say, designed to permit the greatest free-flow of opinion possible. Participants resisted any attempt to elect leaders or a body that could represent the occupations and assemblies themselves (Hughes 2011; Micó and Casero-Ripollés 2013). That such a sentiment was shared across the many occupations taking place is significant. Without reference to an ideology or blueprint many of these initiatives came to the conclusion that they wished to avoid the trappings of representation and representative politics, leaders, politicians, bureaucracy and everything else associated with the current political order. The result was a predictably demanding political practice. Meetings could go on for hours and days before some sort of resolution of a particular problem or before a particular task could be allocated (Taibo 2013). The commitment to consensus made this process even more laborious, as with a simple gesture of crossing one's arms over one's head a single individual could block any decision, a practice that was quickly picked up on by those hostile to the protest or those who wanted them to fail. Nevertheless, the longevity of many of these assemblies and occupations, some of which ran for months, is also telling. Activists were loath to give up the directly democratic form of the assembly. The assembly was, as it were, the *gold standard* for decision-making and for facilitating the participation of ordinary people in the mobilizations.

By 2013 the assemblies had become episodic rather than permanent features of life in Spain's public squares. This is not to say that the assembly had been rejected as a key part of the mobilization. On the contrary, the idea of the assembly as the gold standard remained vivid and real even for those who no longer participated in them. This was marked by the fact that a number of political parties went on to

109

adopt the open assembly form, or 'Circles', as a mechanism of facilitating discussion and deliberation – precisely because it resonated with ordinary people. Clearly the idea of an open forum was enough of an attraction in itself to overcome certain objections concerning the practicality of the assembly for decision-making. Nevertheless, a wider discussion ensued amongst the participants in 15M about how to effect a change in elite behaviour and pave the way for more significant reforms in Spain's economic and political structures. How could a mobilization of the discontented actually make an impact? How could it remain true to its participatory character, and yet become an effective political force? What tools could citizens use to generate change?

On this point activists divided along an axis familiar in the history of organizational politics: between those who argued for the need to organize through a political party and those who wished to stay outside and beyond the mainstream electoral process. On the other hand, the terms and conditions dictating which side of the divide activists took were to be revealing of the changing nature of the status of representation and representative politics.

15M and non-affiliated activism

As we know from previous discussion, many activists in contemporary democracies are doubtful about the virtue of joining political parties. For them political parties are part of the problem, not part of the solution. Many activists in Spain regard the party system as complicit in economic crisis, in ensuring that power is monopolized by the few for the benefit of the few. For them parties are anathema and to be avoided at all costs. Better to find ways of intervening concretely, directly, immediately, to prevent injustice and to protect the victims of the crisis from further misery. Traditionally, 'street' activists have contrasted such forms of activism with party-based activism, which they see as subject to the needs of self-serving elites, whether of the left or the right. A brief account of some prominent groups will give a flavour of the styles of activism practised by non- or anti-party activists in contemporary Spain.

One of the higher-profile groupings is the *Plataforma Afectados por la Hipoteca* (PAH).[3] PAH is a decentralized or grassroots organisation set up to defend those threatened with eviction from their property owing to non-payment of mortgages, a particularly pressing problem in the Spanish context, where banks were encouraged to make up for

110

their losses by recovering assets and selling them on. It's primarily a campaigning body, but also a skill and knowledge share cooperative operating social centres in the major towns and cities of Spain. Some activists are lawyers working on a *pro bono* basis. Others offer counselling skills; others organize support group meetings, demonstrations and petitions to be presented to representatives, judges, the media and external bodies. All are volunteers.

The best known PAH activist is Ada Colau, based in the Barcelona office of the organization. Colau shot to fame on the back of an appearance at a televised Parliamentary hearing where she accused the political class of complicity in inflicting hardship on thousands of ordinary citizens by the banks, many of which had been bailed out by taxpayers' money. The speech was uploaded to YouTube, attracting several hundred thousand viewings within weeks.[4] Colau's Facebook page was swamped with followers, and overnight she became a familiar face in Spanish politics. In recognition of her efforts on behalf of the evicted, she was awarded the European Citizen's Prize by the EU in 2013, a pointed gesture intended to indicate to the Spanish political class the EU's displeasure with how they were handling the crisis.[5] Colau has become another example, with Beppe Grillo and others, of the leader as *anti-politician*, an exemplary figure whose prominence is due to their tapping into a well-spring of disillusionment and anger at the 'politicians'. PAH's popularity, and the popularity of Colau, are due, so it seems, to their studied rejection of mainstream politics in favour of attending to people's real and immediate needs.

The *Iai@asflautas* (or 'Old Hippies') is a popular citizens' initiative composed of retired and older activists who use direct action methods to draw attention to the myriad inequities and injustices of Spain's austerity politics.[6] Many are former members of political parties who have resigned or moved on owing to the well-documented corruption and incompetence of party elites. They blockade or occupy banks, mount pickets outside the offices of politicians and organize protests and demonstrations to draw attention to corrupt or unethical policies, all the while wearing distinctive hi-vis vests to mark them out as a group from other activists. For them the most effective way of making oneself heard is by taking to the streets rather than relying on politicians to raise a topic in Parliament or otherwise speak up for those affected by austerity and recession. They organize regular social events and street parties, and host social centres for meetings and informal gatherings. As noted in the previous chapter, this used to be an aspect of the work of political parties. It was part of the reason they inspired loyalty in many party-based activists. Yet this group had come together because the established parties had become 'bureaucratic', 'distant', 'cut off'. They avoid the division of leaders and led, preferring to decide on actions via assemblies and open meetings. The only stipulation is that one has to be retired or at least 'senior', as the tactics they use (direct action, sit-ins, occupations) play on the unwillingness of the authorities to bully or attack retirees.

Many activists are also involved with various *autonomous initiatives* that set themselves outside and against the mainstream, whether that be considered in political or economic terms. One example is the *Banco Expropriat* (Expropriate Bank) in Barcelona, which collects items from neighbourhoods which are then available for free from a squatted building in the downtown area, also used as a social centre.[7] There are environmental collectives offering local organic produce for sale in poor neighbourhoods, and others which collect food from supermarkets to distribute amongst the needy. Activists involved in initiatives such as these are predictably sceptical about getting involved in 'politics'. Democracy for them is a means of legitimating an unsustainable economy, the exploitation of the poor and the siphoning away of communal resources for the private gain of politicians and their sponsors. They challenge the idea that democracy could be improved by the actions of ordinary citizens. Better to concentrate on everyday initiatives of a practical kind that addressed sustainability, poverty and helplessness head on.

This is just a small sample of the kind of groups and organizations active in the Spanish context. They are in many ways typical of 'poor people's movements' found in many societies (Piven and Cloward 1988). There have always been groups and organizations composed of individuals who want to make a direct contribution to the alleviation of injustice, or who feel that their energies are better spent in terms of the practical and immediate alleviation of suffering than working for a political party. What is nonetheless striking about these contemporary Spanish groups is their alienation from the mainstream political process. They are not 'monitoring' democracy. Nor are they 'participating' or 'joining in'. As organizations they don't have grand plans, ideologies or blueprints for a better world. What they share is a keen sense that the existing system has failed, lost credibility, and that immediate and practical action is needed to avert a human as well as political and economic catastrophe.

Back to the party

Notwithstanding the impact of direct action in the form of assemblies, protests and demonstrations in raising the political temperature in Spain since 2011, this had not brought about a change in the behaviour of elites. Many of those involved in the mobilizations therefore reached the conclusion that the only way of transforming the political dynamic was by challenging political elites directly via the electoral system. This in turn implied the need to organize political parties. However, as we shall see, these were to be parties with a difference.

Since 15M there has been an explosion in the number of political parties, some 490 or so since 2010.[8] This bare fact might be taken to be a source of satisfaction for those who believe that political parties are intrinsic to the healthy functioning of representative democracy. Looking more generally at the kinds of party being created, three functions seem to predominate in thinking about what use a party might serve:

As a mechanism of protest against the political class. As many activists have worked out, occupying public space is unlikely in and of itself to produce change in the mindset or behaviour of elites. What might is a threat to their power and privilege. To take a prominent example, *Escaños en Blanco*, or the 'White Seats' party, was created with the aim of highlighting the bankruptcy of the political class.[9] It runs candidates at elections who promise not to take up their seat in Parliament, thereby leaving a 'white seat' to act as a reminder of the anger and disillusionment of the voting public. White Seats does not have a manifesto or a programme as such. Nor does it offer solutions to the wider economic and social crisis. It sees itself as a single-goal organization: to humiliate the political class. This means that it can present itself as *non-ideological* and 'above the fray'. It also means that its internal organization is simple and relatively non-hierarchical. Since there is no policy to be debated, or programme to be thrashed out, it can concentrate on strategic and tactical issues.

As a way of bringing the 'street' directly into politics. One of the most interesting facets of the current situation is the willingness of avowedly horizontal activists to deploy the party form as a vehicle of mobilization and a means of highlighting the limitations of the present political system. *Podemos* ('We Can'), which scored 8% of the vote in the European elections of 2014 and five seats in the European Parliament, is the most prominent example. It styles itself a party of outsiders committed to 'constructing democracy' from the bottom up, using informal 'Circles' across Spain to inform the basis of its platform. It has no membership or formal barriers to participation, instead seeing itself as a vehicle for ordinary citizens to express themselves unencumbered by the usual trappings of party affiliations.

Partido X: Partido del Futuro is another initiative of self-identifying 'horizontals' seeking to make a break with the legacy of the mainstream parties.[10] The goal of the party is to create the social and political basis for a second, more democratic, transition. By voting for Party X, it claims, one is taking part in a referendum on Spain's political future with a view to its radical transformation towards autonomous and decentralized forms of power, what the party terms *democracia y punto* – 'Democracy. Full Stop'.[11] It's a party intended to highlight the inequities of the system of governance, not to govern in its own right. It sees itself as a party not of 15M itself, which it claims cannot be represented, but of that element that wants to deepen the democratic content of the Spanish system so that it engages ordinary citizens actively and at the everyday or street level.

The *Canditatura d'Unitat Popular*, or Popular Unity Candidates (CUP), is, by contrast, a well-established party with a strong regional identity.[12] However, with 15M it has sought to transform itself in the direction of 'the street'. Since 15M, CUP has adopted many of the slogans associated with the Zapatista movement in Mexico, stressing the primacy of ordinary people in the generation of proposals ('*Nosaltres no us representem, vosaltres ens representeu a nosaltres*' – 'It is people who represent themselves to the party, not the party that represents the People'). CUP encourages participation by both members and non-members of the party, holding public assemblies with the idea of promoting an open and transparent style of decision-making. It is also committed to the idea of delegation, as opposed to representation, insisting that those elected to office be recallable by the relevant constituency, paid an average wage and prevented from standing for more than two elections – an echo of Marx's description of the system adopted by the Paris Commune of 1871 (Marx 1996).

Other parties have a similar approach. The *Procés Constituent a Cataluña*, created in 2013, shares the commitment to open, assembly-style decision-making in order to maintain its connection to street activists.[13] At a national level, *Construyendo la Izquierda* ('Building the Left') was established in May 2012 with the goal of harnessing the energy of disaffiliated or 'street' activists in the name of challenging the status quo.[14] EQUO, another new political party, is committed to direct participation in decision making.[15] Created in 2011, EQUO defines itself as a 'shared project' and encourages those interested in the party to participate in the 'EQUO community', a virtual network in which major issues are discussed in open workgroups on 'the environment', 'economy', 'equality' and 'democracy'. *Izquierda Unida* ('United Left'), a traditional party of the radical left, has introduced changes in its political goals and claims in order to connect with activists otherwise attracted to street politics and mobilizations.[16] The message is clear: party politics cannot proceed as before. Parties have to engage. They have to foster trust, support, solidarity. They have to be 'co-owned', with distributed models of power undermining the formation of cliques or bureaucracy. Above all, they have to feel 'horizontal' – of and for 'the street', ordinary people, not 'them': the politicians, the power-seekers, the professionals.

As a means for advancing the project of direct, participatory or 'post-party' forms of direct democracy. The initial hope of many horizontalists of 15M was that enough pressure could be applied through the process of occupations and assemblies to generate significant political change. Once those hopes ebbed, then the conclusion was drawn, reluctantly, that only by participating in the electoral process could the project to radically transform Spain's democracy be advanced. We have already mentioned Party X as one instance of members of 15M generating a political party, but there are others too. Here we can mention initiatives such as *Partido de Internet* (The Internet Party), *Confluencia* (Confluence) and the *Pirata* (the Pirate party).[17]

The *Pirata* is the local branch of the now well-established Pirate movement, which has already enjoyed electoral success in Germany and Scandinavia. The initial inspiration for the Pirate party was the clamping down of pirate and torrent software sites on the internet by authorities seeking to enforce copyright restrictions. However, it has now developed a more substantial 'libertarian' platform in defence of individual liberty on a number of fronts and the right to participate directly in government. Its aim, shared with 'technopolitical' parties such as Party X and the Internet Party, is to dissolve representative and party-based democracy altogether, and replace it with 'liquid democracy'. This would be a form of democracy built on the so-called 'liquid feedback' initiative.[18] The idea is to use P2P technology permitting individuals to choose between acting and speaking for themselves or ceding their input to a delegate, such as an expert, with whose views they agree. The model seeks to foster greater participation by ordinary citizens, whilst protecting the quality of decision-making through offering an enhanced role for experts and those with experience in the relevant policy field. Implicit in this approach is the idea that to move towards more deliberative and participatory models of governance requires a break with the existing practice of representative politics, as opposed to a roll-out of initiatives to complement it of the kind that has become familiar in the discourse of contemporary politics. If participation of citizens is to be meaningful, then this presupposes an end to the privileged position of politicians and parties in the political system.

Party politics – but not as we know it . . .

As the preceding comments imply, the parties currently being created in Spain are quite different in nature and form to the traditional mass party. It will be useful to reflect for a moment on the characteristics of these parties, not least because they help fill out the sketch of the new forms of mobilization presented in the previous chapter. They include the following:

Parties of the ICT generation. Many of these new initiatives are what might be termed *pop-up parties*, after the much commented-on 'pop-up stores' that are now a regular feature of post-recession high streets across the developed world. Pop-up stores are brief-lived, without ornamentation and designed to maximize impact with the shopper in as short a space of time as possible. Similarly, many of these new political parties are quick-fix, temporary initiatives designed quite explicitly to profit from a moment of political crisis to advance a singular agenda. This is not to say that the activists behind such initiatives do not want to create longer-term and more lasting organizations. It is that the cost of organizing is so low that it is possible to create a basic party platform quickly with a couple of key demands, making the detailed fleshing out of a programme or a manifesto a matter for a later date. Within days a political party can be set up, a logo created, with certain key demands or key issues expressed via a Facebook page. It is in the nature of such evanescent political organizations that they can disappear just as quickly as they emerge. Politics in such a context resembles a mushroom field. Parties pop out of the ground, survive or die just as quickly as they were created. Political experimentation becomes the new norm. Some initiatives will succeed and others will fail.

'Cheshire Cat' initiatives. The primary purpose of many of the new parties is to achieve a singular goal, the realization of which would make them redundant or obsolescent. The goal of the White Seats party is to humiliate the political class. With the achievement of this objective it will apparently disappear. Even those committed to a more expansive programme see their initiatives as of limited duration. Activists attached to Party X are clear that they see the party as a temporary organization designed to provoke a crisis in the political system leading to constitutional change. They didn't want to commit to establishing a permanent party with offices, bureaucracy, leaders and all the other trappings associated with a political party. Techno-political parties like the *Pirata* look forward to the abolition of representative politics and political parties in favour of direct participation in governance. The idea of these parties is to create a *resonance*, an intervention in the political field of such force that it leads to useful change.

Parties with limited ambit claims. Traditional political parties are expected to have a developed position concerning every aspect of social policy, whether that is housing, education or immigration. They have a 360 degree perspective often built from a comprehensive ideology or developed vision of how we should live. A characteristic of the new parties is that they offer a *partial or incomplete view*. They have a clear view about *certain* aspects of the current situation that they wish to see addressed. But few of the new parties have anything like a comprehensive worldview or ideology. They have a 180 degree perspective, or a 90 degree perspective, or less. What we can infer is that offering a comprehensive alternative is seen as much less important than highlighting a particular *deficiency* they wish to see addressed. We should be animated by corruption amongst the political class (White Seats), or the censorship of the Internet (Pirates and Internet Party), or Catalonian independence (CUP). As for the rest, housing, education, and so on, discussion on these matters can be left until later, left until *this particular matter* has been addressed.

Parties against representation. The new parties are *anti-representative* in the sense of rejecting the hierarchical structure and discourse of traditional political parties. The latter seek to promote a particular worldview and to deliver the programme or manifesto presented at election time. Some individuals rise to great prominence and public recognition. They become representatives of the party, and beyond that of the membership and electorate that identify with the party.

The new political parties have rejected this model. Indeed if there is one characteristic that unites these initiatives, it is the rejection of the figure of the 'politician' along with the idea of the party as a vehicle for individuals to assume leadership positions, to become representatives.

This leads to some interesting puzzles. Clearly one of the reasons for the success of *Podemos* in the 2014 European elections was the rise to prominence of Pablo Iglesias, a garrulous but charismatic academic who forms part of the leadership troika of the party. His witty and condescending put-downs of his political rivals resonated in the media, and gave focus to *Podemos*' campaign. On the other hand, *Podemos* stands against the political mainstream and the cult of politicians. In an echo of Marx's and Lenin's recommendations with respect to the rigorous control of delegates, those elected to the European Parliament have agreed to take no more than a 'workers' wage' and to remain answerable to the Circles. But if the success of *Podemos* is down at least in part to Iglesias, shouldn't it try to push him further forward to garner more support? Doesn't his example illustrate the conundrum of 'horizontal' politics – that even when focused on participation, the figure of the representative, the politician, is needed to connect to the wider electorate?

Elsewhere, White Seats will run with named candidates, but it makes it a condition of nomination that candidates promise not to take up their seats in the event that they are elected. Other parties, such as CUP, have recently committed themselves to the principle that candidates can only present themselves for two elections at most, thereby distancing themselves from the practice common in Spain, as elsewhere, of politicians seeking serial re-election. The discourse of all the parties is noticeably antipathetic towards the identification of any individual as a potential or actual leader. These are all self-styled 'parties without politicians' in the Latin American mould – or *anti-party parties* (Genosko 2003).

The party as political tool. It follows from this assemblage of characteristics that party activists (with the exception of CUP) display relatively *low levels of emotional investment* in the party. The contrast with the trajectory of traditional political parties is stark. To be a member of a political party during its heyday in the early to middle of the twentieth century was, for many, an immersive experience. The deeper the ideological cleavages within society, the deeper one's attachment to one's own political party tended to become. The new political parties are, by contrast, 'marriages of convenience' –

118

or perhaps even 'one-night stands'. To invoke Micheletti's analysis, activists shop around for affinities and relationships that match their own analysis. The relationship to political parties is often instrumental and unemotional. It would be a great mistake to read this gesture as implying that today's party activists are selfish or self-absorbed. Rather, it is they have their own views on the nature of the crisis and the best way of addressing it. They aren't beholden to an ideology, a particular organization, a party identity, that they had perhaps inherited or grown up with. The party is a particular kind of tool or lever for achieving certain ends. No more, no less.

In Spain we are therefore seeing the *pragmatic instrumentalization* of the party form itself, and its transformation from a vehicle for representing people, to a mechanism for *creating resonances*. For activists the party is one expression of political possibility; but it is far from being the only one. Indeed, as the comments above indicate, there remains a residual suspicion of the party form itself. This means that the attachment to the party is contingent and mediated by other factors of a strategic and tactical kind. Not only is the level of attachment to the parties low, but the amount of energy that activists are prepared to dedicate to the party in order to see it succeed is measured. There is an acceptance that contemporary initiatives, now *including* political parties, succeed or fail according to whether or not they resonate with the public. Success and failure are dependent not on the amount of work party members themselves put in to building the organization, but rather on the attractiveness and immediacy of the key message.

On the basis of what we see happening in Spain, it is clear that those who fear the decline and indeed the disappearance of political parties within representative democratic systems can be confident that the party is not 'over'. Indeed, in the face of the proliferation and multiplication in terms of the number and form of parties in crisis-afflicted societies such as Spain, one is tempted to invert the sentiment and argue that *the party has only just begun*. Or perhaps it is that we find ourselves in a new 'party' without having realized it. We have left the cosy familiarity of 'cartels', monopolies and duopolies, and found ourselves in an unruly, noisy *street party*. Political analysts might not like what they hear, or they might strain to make out the words, but that doesn't mean to say it's not 'music'.

119

The new 'party-based democracy'

As we have been documenting, the basic coordinates of political life in advanced democracies are changing rapidly (Bauman 1999; Hay 2007; Rosanvallon 2008; Keane 2009). They include the decline of traditional ideologies, the decline of the political party as the bearer of a redemptive or emancipatory project, and an increased antipathy towards politicians as privileged actors or agents in the political process, towards mainstream or official politics generally. As is clear from Euro-barometer and other polling, this has not diminished our attachment to the value of democracy as such. So the issue is whether phenomena such as the proliferation of new actors, including NGOs, 'citizens' initiatives', celebrities, DIY politics, direct action, altermedia, transnational flows of people, ideas, movements, are really a threat to democracy or the basis for a new kind of democracy. The assumption has been that these latter phenomena would further undermine the political party, leading to its decline and perhaps disappearance (Mair and Van Biezen 2001; Ankersmit 2002; Whiteley 2011; Van Biezen. 2012).

If the example of Spain is anything to go by, the evidence suggests that this is unlikely to be the case, even where tendencies towards the disintegration of political parties are felt to be keenest, that is, in societies afflicted by serious economic and political crisis. On the other hand, what is also obvious is that reading these developments as equating to the renewal or rebirth of the traditional mass party would also be wide of the mark. What we are seeing, rather, is the emergence and proliferation of a form of political party that is consonant with the individualized, post-representative styles of politics we documented in the previous chapter. This in turn means that *party-based democracy* is also changing. On the basis of the analysis above, we can summarize the chief developments in the following way:

The principal objective of the new parties is less to seek power than to draw our attention to deficiencies or shortcomings in the nature and practice of representative democracy. One of the key slogans of 15M is ¡*Democracia Real YA!* (Real Democracy Now!). What the slogan flags is a belief that the existing democratic process has become 'fictive' and designed to serve the needs of the elite, not ordinary people. It isn't that Spanish citizens wish to do away with democracy, but that they want democracy to be true to the ideal of a self-governing community, as opposed to a government of and for the rich, or a 'zombie democracy'. Activists had hoped that occupying

120

public spaces and developing 'autonomous' practices would in and of themselves have an impact on the imagination of both the wider public and the elites, somehow forcing a change in democracy. These actions certainly succeeded in bringing these issues into the public sphere; but the realization took hold that protest may not be enough. Parties were formed to continue the struggle to reimagine and reconfigure the institutions and practices of democracy and in particular the electoral system, held by many in Spain to be complicit in maintaining a corrupt duopoly. Here we find an analogy with developments across Europe and elsewhere, for example with the Five Star Movement in Italy and the WikiLeaks party in Australia. These are protest parties whose rationale is to draw attention to the deficiencies of actually-existing democracy and to inspire debate as to how best to address them.

The new parties are less concerned about developing a popular base or membership than creating a resonance that will impact the political field. In the classical model of representative democracy, political parties grow out of the ambition, initially often shared by just a few individuals, to defend the interests, needs and desires of a particular constituency in the electorate. There follows a period of gestation of the party, where supporters are sought, new members are canvassed, funds are acquired, influence is established and reach is developed. As the history of the major parties in advanced democracy shows, this can take years, even decades, of painstaking work.

This is not how the new parties work. Typically, a new party is created on the basis of a Facebook page or through social media, followed by a call-out to interested individuals and groups to affiliate and get involved. Those who make the call-out are seeking an immediate sense of whether their concerns are shared by others. It is the speed of the response that is vital, as the occupations, flash initiatives, assemblies and other forms of immediate action organized by social media attest. The viability of many of these phenomena is measured not in years and decades, but in hours and days. If the initiative resonates, if it is clear through *likes*, *retweets* and *favouriting* that others share the same concerns, then the next steps are made, whether that be in terms of registering a party or suggesting an initial meeting or assembly. If it doesn't, then the initiative withers, and the activists move on. Even as a party establishes itself, the number of actual paid-for members is irrelevant. What is important is the deepening of the resonance amongst the wider population. Is the Facebook page gathering 'likes'? Are the relevant hashtags becoming embedded in the consciousness of activists, citizens, the media? Are people talking about the initiative? Are people turning up to events? Is there *momentum*?

The shift from durable, lasting forms of political organization and initiatives towards evanescent, impermanent and immediate styles of political interaction is mirrored in the nature and form of new political parties. Political scientists and activists have long seen a category difference between direct or DIY politics and the kind of politics that we associate with political parties (Diani and Eyerman 1992; Della Porta and Diani 1998; Day 2004; Mertes and Bello 2004; Castells 2012). This reflects the characteristics of traditional mass political parties touched on above. In previous decades it took a long time to organize a political party. It required a huge amount of energy and enthusiasm to launch an organization, to seek funds, to establish offices and establish a solid platform for mobilizing citizens. Now organizing has become 'ridiculously easy' (Shirky 2009). This makes it much more straightforward to gather like-minded people together, to plan together, to initiate events and actions together. The result is that the party is changing dramatically in accordance with changes in the broader ecology of post-representative politics. This is, as noted above, evanescent, liquid, mercurial. Political parties will come and they will go from election to election, making our connection to them and to what they 'represent' much less secure than the kinds of affiliation and affinity associated with the traditional model. Political parties are just another tool in the repertoire of means by which we can make *ourselves* heard, let off steam, seek to make a difference, get involved, act, and indeed 'participate'. Where once parties dominated, now they are just one more way in which we as individual citizens can seek to influence, query, agitate, transform.

The new political parties are better conceptualized as part of 'counter-democracy' (Rosanvallon) or 'monitory democracy' (Keane) than as part, potentially at least, of the apparatus of the state and governance. As already discussed, the initial motivation as well as rationale for many new political parties, certainly in Spain, is as a way of disrupting the mainstream democratic process and drawing attention to its limitations and deficiencies. Members of these parties are reluctant to see themselves as potential members of government, even as members of a coalition or alliance. This raises the interesting question of what would happen in the event that one or a number of such parties drew a sufficient number of votes to be confronted with the prospect of governing. As the electoral success of Beppe Grillo's Five Star

Movement (5SM) in the 2013 Italian general election and *Podemos* and *Syriza* in the European elections of 2014 illustrates, the scenario is not at all far-fetched. Such is the degree of disaffection amongst the electorate of many European countries, and we could probably add electorates in many other countries of the world, that it is becoming at least conceivable that parties seeking a significant break with the substance and form of traditional parties may make significant headway in electoral terms.

The fate of 5SM is revealing in this respect. The self-image of the party or movement is that of the outsider (Bordignon and Ceccarini 2013). When confronted with its own success, it was almost as if the movement was paralysed and unable to deal with the transition from a posture of protest and disaffection to one of governance. Will it need to reinvent itself in order to cross the line from post-representative to representative organization? Must it as it were repeat the pattern of the past, and devolve power to 'politics' and 'politicians'? Or are we on the cusp of some new mode of politics that transmits some of this anti-representative, horizontal, participatory, networked energy into a genuinely reforming political initiative?

Conclusion

Case studies are intended to illuminate general trends and tendencies. The trap of case studies is that they contain their own idiosyncrasies – and distort rather than illustrate the overall picture. Spain is no doubt an idiosyncratic case in many respects, and there may be those who wonder about the relevance of what has been going on in Spain for other societies such as the US, the UK or indeed Australia, where this author finds himself. In particular it will be objected that Spain has just been through a paralysing crisis, one that brought into question the very legitimacy of Spanish democracy. Yet democracy doesn't take place in a vacuum. Spain is far from the only country touched by profound crisis after the GFC. Many of the styles of mobilization had a copycat effect across other parts of the world, including the US, the UK and even Australia, a country that famously escaped the GFC. And other countries that have not been through the same degree of economic crisis, such as Brazil and Turkey, nonetheless have witnessed similar kinds of political mobilization. Of course the GFC is a profound trigger of protest, but so are Facebook, Twitter, Weibo and the plethora of new devices and ways of organizing opened up by ICT.

What seems to be a better way of thinking about the Spanish case is that it shows, albeit in an accelerated or perhaps exaggerated manner, how certain trends and tendencies remarked upon elsewhere in the book are changing the nature and form of politics in liberal democracies. What in particular they show is the consequence of the individualization of politics on patterns of *affinity, identification and mobilization*. The term *Indignados* is an excellent expression of this change. The disaffected, the angry, 'the 'pissed off', do not map neatly onto sociological categories, class categories, existing typologies. They are, rather, a 'lumpen' expression of unrepresentability. The attachment to the assembly form further amplifies this sense of ordinary people fed up with the mechanisms of representative politics, and with the business of being signed up for and incorporated into other people's schemes, blueprints and rationalities, whether of the left or the right. Recuperating one's own voice was clearly uppermost in the minds of many who participated in the assemblies and even many of those who did not, as the extraordinary approval ratings for the *Indignados* attests (FnfEurope 2013). Once hope in the transforming power of the assemblies waned, so the search for other tools for achieving the same end went on. Direct action, autonomous initiatives, a million little gestures of recuperation and the reimagining of the political party as a vehicle of a sharply *individualized* political practice.

Mobilization has changed. Political parties have changed. Priorities have changed. Citizens in many advanced democracies, and elsewhere, are less impressed by representative politics, representation, politicians. Of course they feel let down by leaders, particularly in those societies still suffering the after effects of the GFC. But what is also telling is the lack of willingness to follow the *would-be* leaders, the saviours of the left, of 'the People', of 'counter-hegemonic projects'. More 'politicians'. More rhetoric. Fewer opportunities to make one's own voice heard. But if we are increasingly reluctant to be represented, where, we need to ask, does this leave democracy? What of democracy after representation? What of ¡*Democracia Real YA!*?

— 6 —

DEMOCRACY AFTER REPRESENTATION

It's been a long journey, but we have finally arrived at our destination, coincidentally also our point of departure: the crisis of representative politics and what it means for democracy. To recall the themes that we were looking at in introducing the topic, we noted a widespread, if not universal, anguish about the future of representative democracy owing to a decline in the variables used to measure the health of the system. We have become reluctant voters, particularly as regards supranational or subnational elections, though we can spring to life when 'it seems to matter' (Wessels 2011). We are markedly less inclined to join political parties, though we seem to be developing a taste for creating our own micro-parties, pop-up parties, protest parties. We trust politicians less than at any time in the past, and less than virtually every other profession, including the usual suspects: second-hand car salesman, journalists and lawyers. Our interest in mainstream or electoral politics is in sharp decline. We know less and care less about our representatives. A plague on 'politics' and 'politicians'.

In light of such scepticism about representative politics, it is, as we have noted, little surprise to find that political scientists and commentators are despondent about prospects for democracy. Not everyone agrees with Keane that democracy is 'dead' (*The Life and Death of Democracy*, 2009). Indeed not even Keane does; but the minor industry of books and articles addressing the matter of the decline of democracy, the crisis of democracy, the end of democracy, tells its own story. 'Endism' is in vogue and the 'end of democracy' narrative is a powerful one.

My own intuition is that there is something suspect in this image of decline based on the waning appetite of citizens to engage in politics in favour of the consolations of introspective and personal pursuits. If anything, the reverse is the case: we seem to be entering a new period of citizen activism, much of it directed at 'the system' and the practice of representation. So the antipathy towards 'politics' and 'politicians' is not just a function of apathy or a waning of interest in politics, though apathy is certainly a powerful countervailing presence in contemporary society. It is also found amongst the politically active, the politically literate, amongst those who are keen to make a difference in some way or other. Hence my suggestion that we should see the decline of representative politics less as the decline of *politics* and more as a decline in the aura and purchase of *representative* forms of politics. To think in images for a moment, it might be less that the water has drained out of the bath, and more that the water has gone cold – cold as far as politicians and parliaments are concerned. But there's still plenty of water in the bath. Politics hasn't drained away, and in certain respects, as otherwise despairing commentators such as Matthew Flinders are right to point out, the opportunities for doing politics, being political and getting engaged in politics, however defined, are greater, perhaps far greater, in certain contexts than they have ever been (Flinders 2012). We just haven't made the switch yet, as analysts, as commentators, indeed as actors, to what this *means*.

This still leaves us with a last puzzle to resolve: what about democracy? Where does this waning interest in the politics of the 'politicians' leave democracy? Doesn't the 'end' of representation mean the end of democracy – or democracy as we know it?

The 'end' of representative democracy

Representative democracy and representative politics were, as we have documented in Chapter 2, the products of a particular moment in time: the emergence of the modern nation state from feudalism, a period that traverses the mid-seventeenth century and culminates in the upheavals of the late eighteenth and early nineteeenth centuries. It can be summarized in the following way:

- a system of political authority over a defined geographical territory with (according to Weber) the state exercising a monopoly over the use of legitimate violence – the nation state;
- a formal separation between the state and civil society or the people;

126

- a system of regular elections to determine who will represent citizens;
- freedom of speech and expression; basic political equality.

Many politics textbooks would include some graphic representation of this system in terms of a pyramid showing those governing or in charge at the top, with some intermediate bodies such as interest and lobbying groups in the middle and with the electorate at the 'bottom'. Some of the diagrams would also show arrows indicating the direction of power and authority. They show that power in a representative democracy doesn't just flow from top to bottom, but involves a relationship of *accountability*, ensuring that the bottom also exercises power over the top on the basis of elections and other safeguards of the public interest. It's a simple image to grasp. It's no doubt because of its simplicity that it is immensely difficult to abandon, which is why we have been referring to the idea of representative politics as a paradigm. The image of the self-governing 'pyramid' is, however, becoming less useful as a way of describing the nature of democracy under contemporary conditions. Developments over the past half-century are eroding its key features, transforming the political terrain. Key changes include the following:

Complex territorialities. The image of the nation state as an autonomous entity with clearly defined borders and a clearly defined realm over which the state presides is progressively less applicable to many nation states (McGrew and Lewis 2013). There are few states that can afford to ignore the edicts of a growing superstructure of international and global bodies such as the United Nations, the World Trade Organization, the International Criminal Court and the International Monetary Fund. But this is just the tip of the iceberg. In virtually every field of activity there is now an important role for international bodies who in turn define rules, norms and procedures over a kaleidoscopic array of subjects. Whilst it remains some sort of option for the leaders of nation states to decide whether and to what extent to respect the strictures of bodies such as these, in reality the price for not doing so is too much to bear for all but global hegemons such as the US, or states such as North Korea and Iran untroubled by 'rogue' or pariah status. For other states, it's a matter of going with the flow in order to reap some benefit as well as avoiding sanction. In addition many countries now find themselves part of some supranational entity that in turn modifies the image of the sovereign territory. European countries may be part of the EU, the euro, the European

Trade Area, the Schengen Agreement, and sometimes all the above. Each of these arrangements undermines the image of sovereignty at the heart of the post-Westphalian image of the state, as we saw in the previous chapter with respect to Spain.

Other parts of the simple geometry of the nation state are similarly under pressure. Saskia Sassen paints a compelling portrait of the rise of the global city as a key part of the emerging contemporary topography (Sassen 1996, 2006). As she documents, there are now forty or so mega-cities whose prominence and position in the global economy are such that they can be said to occupy a quite distinct layer of power and authority of their own. She argues that global cities disrupt the easy opposition between the 'national', on the one hand, and the 'global', on the other. We could go on to discuss the importance of the *region* or *province* in states such as India and China (Markusen 1987; Amin 2004). Again, the image of the geographically distinct community presided over by a relatively simple political geography finds itself increasingly at odds with the emerging or perhaps re-emerging reality of complex multi-scalar territorialities or 'multipolarities' (Wade 2011).

Complex sovereignties. It is not just the sense of the integrity of the territory that is increasingly under pressure, but also the idea of power and thence sovereignty as something that can be easily mapped in terms of the relationship between the top and bottom of a line diagram or pyramid (Sassen 1996; Chayes and Chayes 1998). Whilst it may suit many discursive strategies to emphasize the sovereignty of the state, not least to offer the impression that 'we', however defined, are in control of our own destiny (or potentially so), power is progressively evolving in terms of much more complex relationships than this image suggests. This is not the same as saying that the state is powerless, or that it doesn't matter, which is sometimes implied in the 'death of the state' literature. Notwithstanding Foucault's admonition to 'cut off the head of the king', the state is still a crucial repository of power and indeed force in the contemporary world (Foucault 1980). Just ask the citizens of the Ukraine or Tibet or countless other subject, satellite or vassal states living next door to heavily armed hegemons whether state power has become an irrelevancy. What is more the case is that the state is itself a much more complex entity than it was even a few decades ago. The contemporary state is composed of vast, complex bureaucracies covering defence, health, education, social security, interlocking and interweaving in a knot of varying and often hybrid structures tying together private interests and public bodies. The state is also competing with other sources of power and authority, not the least of which are powerful corporations, money markets, derivatives traders, international bodies, religious groups, transnational networks, NGOs, the global media. Many such organizations have the capacity to mobilize people, to influence them. They can create new relations of power as well as impacting existing relationships. They can often circumvent the state, make its life easier or more difficult, engage as actors in their own right, and indeed 'represent' (or try to), providing a further layer of complexity to the image discussed above.

Complex (non-/post-)identities. Representative democracy was the product of the modern imagination, and intrinsic to that imagination is the idea of the self-determination of peoples. So the rationale of representative government is to permit an already identifiable People to govern itself in accordance with its own values, beliefs and interests. Recognizing that the creation of a People was an indispensable accessory to making the representative claim work, modern nation states have seen it as their task to maintain a clear national identity, or, as has often been the case, to construct one in the face of the unruly persistence of varieties of indigenous, tribal, regional and local identities that threaten to disrupt the image of a unified People as the author of sovereignty (Rae 2002). Today, that process finds itself unravelling in the face of globalization, transnational migration and a communicative abundance that facilitates access to a profusion of cultural products from all over the world. We are more than ever able to 'pick and mix' our own cultural attachments in a way that would have been much more difficult even a generation ago.

The result is the increasing *hybridization* of contemporary societies, the problematization of national identity and therefore of the People as the subject of representative politics. Rosanvallon goes as far as to note, with a Gallic shrug, that the People is '*introuvable*' – lost, gone, and with it the idea of representation as a process that completes the circle of authorization between the People and its representatives (Rosanvallon 2002). Authorization appears incomplete, fractured, resulting in a gap into which other kinds of claim can emerge, whether it be the claims of clerics, celebrities or activists (Saward 2011). Politicians are now *one kind* of representative; but they struggle in increasing degree to represent the whole, 'the generality'. 'The People', a monument of the nineteenth-century imaginary, is progressively eroded by flows of migrants, ideas, cultures, products, media. In its place emerge complex, heterogeneous, 'disjunctural' societies composed variously of the represented, the unrepresented

129

and the unrepresentable, the latter an increasingly important element of the mix (Appadurai 1996).

These changes do not impact in uniform fashion around the world, and no doubt will chime to a greater or lesser degree depending on which society one is talking about. What we are noting are trends and tendencies, the shifting of tectonic plates, as opposed to the existence or otherwise of a particular state of affairs. Nevertheless, it is these trends and tendencies that underpin a particular image of decline that we find repeated in the works of Hay, Keane, Della Porta, amongst numerous others:

- the loss of the sense of 'sovereignty' – or the capacity of states to govern themselves;
- the loss of the aura of national politicians able to shape policy in accordance with commitments made to the electorate at election time;
- the loss of the sense of being represented by politicians, who are increasingly required to conform to the views and needs of multiple actors and agencies both internal and external to the state;
- an overall sense of loss of power, loss of control, waning influence and the erosion of democracy.

It is this set of conclusions that underpins the 'emptying bath' image invoked above. The perception is of politics draining away, leaving a rump of politicians no longer beholden either to their own parties or indeed to their own electorates, but rather to a plethora of agents, bodies, organizations, chivvying away, often unreported behind the scenes, to deliver outcomes that may have little to do with the mandate they received from the electorate. Crouch's term 'post-democracy' catches the atmosphere well. As he describes it, politicians have become detached from 'politics', from debate, contestation (Crouch 2004). They have becomes proxies for powerful interests often located beyond or outside the nation state. The image of the politician as having a direct connection to the electorate and being held accountable to it has gone, and with it the democratic content of politics. Keane's idea of 'monitory democracy' offers further food for thought, emphasizing the increased role of non-elected public and private bodies in pressing against the skein of politics, harassing politicians and generally reducing the sense of politics as a public enterprise in favour of a system of governance that has to be 'monitored', 'audited', 'watched' (Keane 2011). It's a long way from the image of lofty ideals, noble sentiments, collective endeavour, that underpins classic accounts of what democracy should be about, not least those such as Urbinati who continue to defend representative democracy against its many critics on grounds that it sets in motion a continual dialogue between representatives and the represented (Urbinati 2011). Rosanvallon agrees in large measure with these descriptions, adding that we have entered an era in which whatever sense of connection once existed between electorate and politicians has been diluted to the point where, increasingly, it makes little sense to describe the electorate as being represented by politicians at all (Rosanvallon 2008). The bath seems to be emptying.

From representation to resonance

There's no doubt a lot of truth in these descriptions, and they certainly chime with sections of the public. Hence the appeal of a certain brand of populism that seeks a return of politics back to the 'People', that seeks withdrawal from the denationalizing forces of the EU and global markets, and that seeks to turn back the 'tide' of immigration. Certainly if one's view of democracy rotates around the words and deeds of those elected to the 'highest office of the land', then the prognosis is bleak. Whatever respect citizens once had for politicians and the political class is fast disappearing. Whether the blame lies with the media, citizens or politicians, the aura is fading. It is the figure of the non- or anti-politician that is in the ascendant.

On the other hand, often the assumption in the 'end of democracy' thesis is that it is a decline in our engagement and interest in politics that provides at least part of the explanation. Hence the target of Flinders' *Defending Politics* (2012) which picks up from Hay's *Why We Hate Politics* (2007) in identifying us citizens as at least partly complicit in the story of decline. Yet the decline of democracy is not caused by a decline of *politics* per se. On the contrary, there is an awful lot of politics about. The problem is that it doesn't necessarily conform to the *kind* of politics that is helpful in maintaining the image of a healthy and vibrant representative democracy. Representative politics is in decline, both in terms of a politics that is helpful to the election of representatives and in terms of a distinct style or mode of engaging with others as 'speaking for'. But this doesn't necessarily equate to the end or decline of democracy; rather it signifies the shift away from a neat, predictable form of politics towards a different logic or *economy* of politics. How might this be expressed? Representative politics embraces what we might call a *linear view* of the political process. Get organized, present for elections, get the vote out, win the election, enact policies x, y and z – repeat the above. Linear politics reflects the assumptions discussed above about how politics works. It is above all a question of competing for control over the state, and then using the power of the state to secure a certain vision of equality, justice, the Good Life. The disappointment about the direction in which democratic politics is heading reflects the waning of this easy-to-grasp account of how politics and power work. And because it has been such a dominant way of thinking about politics both on the left and on the right over the past two hundred years, it seems there is nowhere to go but down. If state-centric representative politics doesn't work any more, if it doesn't have purchase on our imagination, then the conclusion is drawn that politics and democracy must both be in decline. But the conclusion is too hasty. It's not capturing the sense of what is happening to politics, and how politics is rapidly changing in relation to the various coordinates described above, which are in turn affecting the scope, nature and form politics takes. Representative politics based on a linear economy is being supplemented, displaced, overtaken, rendered obsolescent, with the emergence of a different kind of 'post-representative' politics based on a different non-linear economy that we have been terming *resonance*.[1] What form does it take?

Creating impetus. Representative politics was the response historically to the difficulty of organizing groups, campaigns, initiatives and ultimately governance. It made a lot of sense to join together with others to create stable enduring organizations to defend the needs and interests of a particular group. High transaction costs, the limited availability of time, the differential skill sets within a group, all pointed towards the kind of organization we have been discussing under the heading representative politics, principally the mass political party and trade unions. The politics of the last two centuries often concerned the advancement of a group or collective identity. It implied the desirability of building scale and capacity in organizational terms. Many citizens readily accepted the desirability and necessity of joining large member organizations in order to safeguard and advance their own interests. Contemporary politics is developing from a different dynamic with a different starting point. As we have noted, often the spark that initiates the desire to act is a shared sense of *injustice*. That sense of injustice might be in relation to the conditions of a group. But it might also be in relation to a particular policy, a breach of certain rights or just a generalized sense of anger, fear

132

or resentment. Whereas it might once have been quite a task to find others who shared that sense of injustice or anger, now, as we have noted, it is *very easy*, and this is having a far-reaching impact in terms of creating political initiative. A few moments Googling, searching Facebook or putting out a hashtag will reveal many others with similar feelings. The next step might be to propose creating a group or holding a meeting, perhaps virtually, to decide what to do – how to *intervene, disrupt, act, influence the political field.*

Creating resonances. The old 'economy' led to the seeking of members for a new group or organization. Political parties drew strength directly from recruiting people who could then help build up the organization, campaign in elections, raise funds or indeed 'man the barricades'. Now that group formation is so easy, the task is very different. It is to create a sense of momentum through generating resonances. In Chapter 4 we documented this economy of resonances and in Chapter 5 we saw how this played out in the Spanish context. A few activists inspired by actions elsewhere propose via social media a set of initiatives to engage ordinary people in a protest against their own government, indeed the political class as a whole. If enough people can be mobilized, then this creates further resonances, hopefully of sufficient strength or *amplification* to have an impact in terms of the way the public perceives issues around corruption, austerity, mortgage arrears, lack of voice.

Resonant politics is based on a 'connective politics' that is rapidly supplanting the mass membership organization in much the same way that the internet is draining the life out of traditional forms of retail (Bennett and Segerberg 2012). Mass parties, like retail stores, cost a lot to maintain. They are resource hungry, whether that resource be money, time or effort. New technologies dramatically reduce the costs involved in organizing and initiate a very different sense of 'activism'. At the same time, it's more hit and miss, more evanescent. But lowering costs means that the barriers to creativity, experimentation, innovation, are lower. There will be many damp squibs, dead internet pages, un-liked Facebook pages, hashtags that dissolve into the virtual fog. But equally there will be other little initiatives that connect, inspire, provoke. Some will create new, more durable micro-organizations, affinity groups, blocs, coalitions and indeed parties. Others will provoke more initiatives. Some of them will be difficult for politicians to ignore. Others will be taken up by those 'monitory' bodies that seek to promote the public interest. Others will be the subject of newspaper campaigns, and lead to the boycotting of goods and services. Some of them will result in the naming or shaming of individuals, politicians, lobbyists. On it goes.

Creating clamour. The test for any style of activism has to be measured in terms of the outcomes it delivers. These outcomes were able to be mapped and measured with great precision as far as linear politics was concerned. A certain number of members is needed for a political party to register; a certain number of votes to win a constituency; a certain number of seats in Parliament in order to guarantee a majority, which will in turn enable a party or a president to propose new legislation in accordance with a programme or manifesto. Easy to understand, easier to study, map, quantify. Resonance doesn't conform to this logic. The aim of many contemporary initiatives is, as it were, to create *clamour* or a sense of indignation, anger or dismay of such a force that it creates effects in terms of the development of new initiatives, new actions, which will in turn shape, impact, alter public perceptions, elite perceptions, media perceptions. Just how many signatures on a petition are needed? How many people on the street? How many occupations, demonstrations, 'likes'? How much noise is needed before office holders think it is the right time to act?

Politicians in democratic societies have always had to be attentive to 'the climate of opinion' in determining which policies to pursue and how. But the matter used to be more straightforward in the past, where there were a limited number of newspapers, public service TV channels and few means of mass communication available for ordinary citizens. In a media-saturated environment where citizens have access to non-elite news and information, where issues and injustices can be tweeted, Facebooked, communicated, in an instant at near-zero cost, and where it is relatively easy to organize, create groups and campaigns, the ecology is transformed, and with it, potentially at least, the impact in terms of public consciousness of an issue. But what is becoming clearer is that resonance implies a different kind of causality and a different model of 'effect' or 'outcome' that traverses borders and boundaries. Some initiatives have an immediate, observable impact in terms of provoking a crisis or emergency that demands a response. Others create much more complex or chaotic effects. How, for example, to map the 'chain of causality' that led to the mobilization of the *Indignados*? Where did it start? Where is it heading? Resonances, social media, street protests – a chaotic interplay of the real and the virtual.

Creating turbulence. As is becoming increasingly evident, the new styles of politics are capable of having effects not just on particular policies or particular practices, but in terms of the viability and legitimacy of governments and even of states. One of the most suggestive illustrations of how the new politics of mobilization has changed potentially at least the balance between citizens and those who govern was in Iceland in 2008 (Castells 2012). Iceland was the first country affected by the credit crunch of 2007 owing to the activity of its banks, which had dramatically overreached themselves in the search for better returns. Iceland went bankrupt. Many citizens lost all or part of their savings and retirement funds. Calls for a mobilization against the Icelandic Parliament went out, which resulted in mass protests ('the pots and pans protests') and occupations in the capital Reykjavik calling for the re-foundation of the Icelandic constitution so as to avoid a similar situation arising in the future.[2] The call was accepted by a political class that was now cornered, humiliated and keen to be seen to redeem itself. Measures were put in place making bankers and politicians more accountable and policies more transparent and open to public view. It was peaceful. It was largely leaderless. It resulted in changes to the constitution and the comportment of elites. But significantly, it also appears to have transformed the comportment of *citizens*, emboldening them to see in their own efforts a way in which democracy could mean something more than mandating others to act on one's behalf, to speak on one's behalf. It could also mean citizens acting, constituting and reconstituting their own system of governance, albeit as 'representative'.

Not all such developments have had a similarly productive result. The mass mobilizations in Spain have yet to produce much in the way of actual change to match the febrile creativity demonstrated by citizens. The same might be said of Turkey, where the ruling elite was rattled by extensive occupations, but without in the end needing to concede too much in order to maintain its grip on power. Until recently, however, it was difficult to imagine mobilizations involving hundreds of thousands of citizens in such countries. Iceland and Spain are both mature democracies with functional representative systems. Turkey is a 'consolidated' democracy without a recent history of mass citizen activism of a kind seen in 2013, not least owing to an oppressive police and state apparatus. Something is changing. Citizens are becoming emboldened as the costs and risks of confronting injustice, corruption, incompetence, reduce.

It's early days for this new phase of ICT-enabled 'citizen activism', but the rapidity with which we are moving from an at least outwardly stable and predictable relationship between governments and people towards one that is more fluid, dynamic and contingent is eye-catching. It's taking us beyond the discrete concerns of 'social movements' as these have often been thought about in the context of democratic societies, that is, as ways in which citizens can bring pressure to bear on representatives to act in relation to a particular issue. It's moving us to a sense of democracy not just as 'constituted' or as a system whose parameters and coordinates can be taken for granted, but as *constituting*, that is, as involving an on-going negotiation and renegotiation of what democracy means – how it works, for whom – between citizens and power holders. The ease of mobilization means that citizens take on the appearance of a democratizing force pressing against the institutions and practices of democracy – an 'outside' able to exogenously influence, shape, mould, the system and *in extremis* to reconstitute it along new lines.

The collision of 'vertical' and 'horizontal'

Assuming for a moment that the economy of politics is changing in the way described here, what then might be the impact of the change on the familiar world of representative democracy?

The transformation of 'party-based democracy'

The decline of the linear model of politics, a politics of ideologies, group interests, clear identities, in favour of a much less organizationally rigid attachment to relatively fluid and evanescent political structures is leading to the detachment of the 'political class' from the politically active part of the citizenry. Political parties that once counted their memberships in the millions are shrivelling to the point where what is left is a core membership supporting a small executive team of ambitious political figures. With the withering of memberships, the ordinary party loyalist is often sidelined in a quest to uncover the famed 'middle ground' where the majority of the votes can be found. Meanwhile politically active citizens explore other means of making themselves heard, including creating their own 'micro-parties'.

As we saw in Chapter 5, there are various different iterations of the micro-party. Some seek to protest against the political class or style themselves as 'anti-politics'. Others are sectional interest group parties. And as we saw in the case of Spain, there are now a range of parties devoted to the issue of political design, and to rethinking what democratic governance means. Many of them take their cue from what they perceive to be the possibilities implied in technological developments and, in particular, P2P governance, twiki initiatives and other kinds of interactive technologies that might facilitate greater involvement by ordinary citizens in decision-making.

There is, then, little threat to the existence of political parties as such under contemporary conditions, and it is difficult to foresee circumstances where political parties become sidelined even through quite radical or far-reaching constituent processes. What we are seeing, however, is a change in the ecology of 'party-based democracy' and in turn the nature of the *form of governance* associated with political parties. Fading from view is the image of party-based democracy as a mechanism whereby the vast majority of the electorate can be expected to be represented on a periodic basis as the major parties take it in turn to have their 'go' at government. In its place is emerging a different kind of contest, one between *parties of governance*, on the one hand, and *parties of protest*, on the other – or between 'insiders' and 'outsiders'.

The new (political) class warfare

The decline of the mass party is, predictably, a worry for political scientists, implying as it does the decline of orderly, predictable and largely quiescent politics in favour of something disorderly (Whiteley 2011; Van Biezen et al. 2012). Too much clamour, noise, instability – a neighbour's barbecue gone wrong. On the other hand, what it presages is a shake-up in the Schumpeterian idea of 'the political class' familiar in the complex monopoly environment of contemporary democracy. Instead of the slow 'rotation of elites', we are evolving a centrifuge spitting out politicians and parties in rapid succession. It's alarming at one level. Change in the basic coordinates of a system often is. But something interesting is going on. At one level, representative politics is 'elite' politics, whether those elites are the grandees of the Tory Party or the *Parti Communiste Française*. Yet it is the very basis of elite politics that is under threat as we move from a slow rotational politics to an evanescent ecology that throws up new parties, organizations and political figures with increasing rapidity. Money still talks; but money alone is less able to drown out the growing clamour and chatter of new initiatives. In addition, party politics is becoming a game that 'Everybody' can play, with interesting results. The Italian general election of 2013 saw an anti-mainstream, anti-political movement, Beppe Grillo's 5SM, attract more votes than any other single party. It was an earthquake, a wake-up call, a sign of a paradigm waning. Grillo's success was due in very large measure to his grasp of the extraordinary mobilizing power of social media. Activists of many different stripes have 'joined the party' in Spain. Indeed the party is now the preferred vehicle for avowedly 'anti-party' elements of the *Indignados*: *Podemos, Partido X*, the *Pirata, Escons en Blanc*. The list goes on. In Australia the process is facilitated by a peculiar electoral system that favours micro-parties standing for Senate election, promoting the proliferation of a new 'awkward squad': the Motorists Enthusiasts Party, the Australian Sports Party and a micro-party I might even vote for myself, the Australian Cyclists Party. Parties were once exclusive affairs with high entry costs; but the doors have been thrown open. Now anyone can join the party.

A redrawing of the relationship between governments, politicians, authorities and citizens now better able to act in 'swarm' or 'crowd' mobilizations

As Rosanvallon and Keane suggest, the move to a 'post-representative' form of democracy should not necessarily be taken as implying that politicians, governments and states are better able to get their own way, as is often implied in the commentary of political scientists worried by the decline in participation in official and mainstream politics (Rosanvallon 2008; Keane 2009). Rather, they are now confronted by a battery of organizations and associations devoted to 'monitoring' their activities and alerting the public to any cause for concern. However, 'post-representation' goes beyond the rather fixed or static relationship implied in the term 'monitory'. Citizens are themselves seeking to get involved, to participate, to become actors in their own right, as opposed to relying on organizations apparently defending the public interest or the interests and needs of particular groups to do it for them. Citizens are getting organized. They are creating micro-initiatives, micro-parties, micro-politics, devoted to harassing and cajoling politicians and challenging particular policies. In certain contexts citizens are becoming emboldened to challenge leaders, governments, states, regimes, directly which for whatever reason have incurred the wrath and anger of subject populations.

That this is taking place in democracies as well as in non-democracies should alert us to the fact that what is taking place here is more than something negative. Democracy, or what has long been taken to be democracy, is itself being challenged or queried when it seems to fall short of the expectations that citizens have of it. And those expectations are changing rapidly. The cosy relationship between political and economic elites was the subject of the mass mobilization in Iceland. The predictable duopoly of the Spanish political system which masked a system of clientelism, cronyism and corruption was the spark for the mobilizations in Spain. The ability of the political elites to impose extra costs on the poorest parts of the population was a cause of extensive and on-going demonstrations in Brazil. Hundreds of thousands march on the streets of Hong Kong to demand better protection from the authorities, more rights, greater participation. Insensitive use of power, lack of transparency, lack of trust: these are still factors held to be causes of introspection and apathy amongst the electorate. Now, increasingly, they are the cause of mobilizations, activisms, new political initiatives seeking a more equal distribution of power and a more involving form of decision-making. Underpinning the shift is the capacity of ordinary people to generate collective power to produce a 'swarm' or 'crowd' effect through ease of communication, in turn facilitating the development of *individualized* forms of interaction of a non-bureaucratic and often leaderless kind.

So to summarize the changes underway:

- We are seeing a context in which power is progressively less the preserve of relatively autonomous nation states to one where power and decision-making are dispersed in a multi-scalar, non-unitary assemblage of actors which include nation states, but also corporations, transnational advocacy groups, NGOs, religious organizations, media groups.
- We are seeing a change in the economy and ecology of politics from one based exclusively or primarily on an 'organized' competition for power involving traditional mass membership parties to a flatter, more evanescent 'dis-organized' politics, the object of which is often to create resonances or 'effects' in the political field.
- We are seeing a transformation of party-based democracy away from the complex monopoly of a small number of mass parties ('the rotation of elites') towards a contest between 'executive teams' (parties of governance), on the one hand, and various pop-up, micro-, protest or anti-party parties, on the other (parties of protest).
- We are seeing a proliferation of non-party activisms, flash

139

activisms, resurgent and sometimes insurgent political initiatives greatly facilitated by ICT.

- We are seeing the erosion of the aura of democracy as 'collective self-governance' to reveal democracy as a contest between those 'below' – an increasingly unrepresentable and occasionally ungovernable mass of citizens acting in groups, organizations, 'swarms'– and those 'above', who govern, rule, possess power.

Post-representative democracy?

So how to frame this emerging image? Why 'post-representative democracy'? What is signified by it? Why don't we just go the whole hog and agree with Colin Crouch that we are living in 'post-democracy'?

Firstly, a note about the term 'post-'. 'Post-' is often used in the humanities to denote a moment of crisis or hiatus in the object following the prefix. The most celebrated – or notorious – use of this prefix is 'postmodernism', a term associated with the work of Jean-François Lyotard, who, as noted in Chapter 4, coined the term the 'postmodern condition' (Lyotard 1984). What he meant was that many of the expectations associated with the modernist standpoint had run aground. Modernism in politics is above all associated with the idea of *progress*, of our lives getting better, or at least potentially better. This would either be towards some final end point or goal such as communism, or just in the sense of an on-going improvement in our standard of living, collective and individual capabilities or sense of flourishing. What Lyotard observed is that we were becoming more sceptical towards 'metanarratives', or stories of how our lives would improve, and less inclined to believe in the redemptive promises of ideologies of whatever hue. 'Postmodernism' was not, then, intended to indicate a time 'after' the modern, or a break which ushers in some new logic or system in the manner in which, say, capitalism is said to follow on from feudalism (Heller and Feher 1988). It marks a moment where a 'paradigm' or narrative wanes, but where the outline of something else that might replace the paradigm is still obscure and difficult to make out. We can't live with it; but nor can we live without it – for the time being. The key point is the sense of *remaining with* as opposed to *leaving behind*. This 'remaining with' is what is captured with 'post-representative democracy' in several key respects.

The end of an aura?

Representative democracy has been the dominant way of thinking about the basis of political order for the past two hundred years. In many respects it still is. It's immensely difficult for political scientists, let alone ordinary citizens, to contemplate a different way of organizing collective life other than through representative practices and procedures. At the same time our view of those who represent us is becoming ever more framed by doubt, scepticism, contempt. Citizens are wearied of politicians, elites and the day-to-day business of 'politics' as this is usually thought about. This in turn gives us an impression of 'crisis'. That there appears to be a crisis should not, however, be taken to imply that representative democracies are about to collapse, which is sometimes the impression given by the commentary (Della Porta's *Can Democracy be Saved?*, 2013). Democracies can carry on functioning even where many profess indifference towards their representatives and competitive elections. One of the aspects of representative democracy that gives it a certain robustness is, paradoxically, that it barely needs us to take part at all. Apathy is not necessarily the enemy of representative democracy, as is often implied in the commentary; it can also be its friend. Apathetic citizens are citizens who can be governed, ruled, taxed, spied on, ordered about and controlled with impunity. Being governed and ordered about hardly conforms to the classical image of democracy as a 'self-governing community of equals'; but this lack of contiguity between the promise and the reality of representation is a problem for political theorists, not elites. In any case the evidence suggests that we are not about to give up on democracy as an ideal. Many of the elements associated with modern democracies retain significant levels of support: independent judiciaries, freedom of speech, civil rights, and so forth. The issue is that we are less inclined to believe that the system of representation *represents*. To deploy Lyotard, the metanarrative that sustained the view that our views somehow inform the choices and decisions of those in power, our representatives, invokes 'incredulity'. As one banner brandished in a protest in Spain puts it: 'This is not a crisis, it is that I do not love you any more' (quoted in Castells 2012: 122).

Hence the ever-diminishing status of politicians. For all the inventive thinking about how exactly representatives represent us, whether it be the trustee model or the principal–agent model or the 'gyroscopic' model, what seems more germane to understanding the normative basis of representation is, quite simply, that it provides a degree of *accountability* for those exercising power. Citizens may be less inclined to feel that they are being represented in any substantive way, but the system of periodic elections at least means – in principle anyhow – that those who wield power can be held to account and voted out. From this point of view, elections are becoming less a moment when individual citizens assert their preference *for* something, so much as a moment when we assert the 'negative' or 'counter-democratic' power of reminding politicians that they depend on us for their own position and privilege (Rosanvallon 2008). Elections are 'pay-back time' for increasingly grumpy citizens.

Reflecting the above, representative democracy is becoming the basis upon which the frustrations of citizens are played out: via micro-parties, anti-party parties, anti-political politicians. The greater the pull of the electoral system for such initiatives, the greater, paradoxically, the system is *affirmed* – albeit negatively. Does any of this represent a threat directly and immediately to the institutions and practices of representative democracy? Not so far. The result in Iceland was the reaffirmation of representative democracy, albeit with better measures to ensure transparency, accountability and the ability to monitor the behaviour of economic and political elites. The march of the pop-up parties in Spain is witness to the view of many within the 15M movement that assemblies and occupations are unlikely in and of themselves to supplant or replace representative bodies and procedures. Better it seems to focus on a second Spanish 'transition' – a more supple, plural, open, system of *representation* than that which ushered in the first. The fire in the belly of Beppe Grillo's initiative waned as it became caught up in the very web of complexity, messiness and intractability it was elected to 'cure'. The examples abound. We are not about to leave representation; rather, we are seeing a querying and questioning of the inheritance of representation – how it works, for whom, by whom – in the hope of moving past the 'fictive' component towards something that is felt to be a 'real' or 'true' representation of democracy.

The long wait for the 'democracy-to-come'

A growing disillusionment with representative democracy has generated a rich literature of other ways in which we might think about and practise democracy, from variants of strong democracy, to deliberative democracy, direct democracy, assembly democracy and now technologically driven variants of 'liquid democracy'. None of them has so far shown signs of being able to generate the momentum needed to present an alternative of a kind that we associate with the transformative ideologies of the nineteenth and early twentieth centuries in the manner of socialism or communism. Nor is there very much reason to think they or some other project, blueprint or ideology will do so in the near future. The hope of those such as Hardt and Negri that contemporary forms of production will in and of themselves bring forward the demand for the self-governance of the 'multitude' might have a certain romantic attractiveness, but it belongs firmly to the 'wishful thinking' school of analysis (Hardt and Negri 2004). The recent improbable nostalgia for 'communism', albeit one purged of connection to communism as an actual historical movement, also speaks to a rejection of present arrangements in favour of something purer, more inclusive and engaging which representative democracy is unable to supply (Badiou 2008; Dean 2009). Ideas like these will find an audience amongst those fed up with present arrangements; but they are short of that vital ingredient to effect change along the lines familiar from the history of ideological politics: *believers*. Žižek might be able to fill the Sydney Opera House for the 'Festival of Dangerous Ideas', but, as the setting denotes, it is *entertainment* his audience craves, not a new gnostic faith.[3]

Representative democracy has proven not only resilient in terms of holding off other models, but able otherwise to recuperate the demand for greater participation in ways that have reinforced the primacy of representative democracy as opposed to posing a possible pathway out of it. Many representative systems now offer increased opportunities to participate in the form of referendums, citizen juries and panels, participatory budgeting, deliberative forums, online polls, and the like. The vast literature on the topic is itself witness to the hope that some political influence and power can be wrestled from elites and placed in the hands of ordinary citizens (Della Porta 2013). The belief that it can may help explain why instead of thinking about alternatives to representative democracy, many are preoccupied with 'renewing' or restoring it, albeit with a healthy dose of 'deliberation' or 'participation'.

Surveying the terrain, however, offers little reason to get excited. The current measures taken are too little, too late: a bandaid on a multitude of problems – financial meltdown, outsourcing, privatization, climate change, resource depletion, inequality. A generalized indifference to such initiatives, well meaning though many of them are, adds to the sense of our being in a 'post-representative' moment as opposed to one where there is a clear choice between 'continuing on as we are' and embracing some quite different or radically redrawn notion of what democracy *might* be. Where are the popular movements calling for more participatory budgeting, citizenship education or deliberative forums? No doubt they exist, but their voice is currently rather feeble, certainly when compared to the noise and clamour of those protesting against corrupt or ineffective regimes, politicians, political parties. For the present we are in-between worlds, visions, concepts. One vision seems exhausted, but difficult to dislodge. Other visions and practices swirl around in a vortex of experimentation, initiatives, contestations and resistances. We live in a kind of hiatus: a world between worlds, unhappy at the present, but uncertain about what a redrawn future might imply. As Žižek himself notes, '[W]ho knows what to do today? There is no Subject who knows, neither in the form of intellectuals nor ordinary people' (Žižek 2012b: 89).

Democracy after 'post-democracy'?

Colin Crouch's term has clearly resonated, and with good reason. It captures the sense of how many experts, commentators and citizens feel about democracy in the wake of the restructuring of the relationship between state and society arising from neoliberal reforms in the 1990s and 2000s in many if not all advanced democracies. The imposition of New Public Management, the outsourcing of many functions previously regarded as integral to the idea of the public realm, and the consequent sense of politics as having little purchase or meaning any more are certainly facets of the present conjuncture. But the idea that this equates to a supersession of democracy – or 'post-democracy' – is to see democracy in only one of its dimensions: as an elite-driven activity. It is becoming clearer that much rests on decisions taken elsewhere other than in Parliament and Congress. They remain important repositories of power, but far from the only ones. Power is becoming more diffuse, complex, multi-scalar. It is no longer – assuming it once was – the monopoly of the state. Political theorists might be reluctant to 'cut off the head of the king', but as the profusion of transnational causes, networks, advocacy groups, testifies, citizens have seen the head roll and are busy chasing after the new hydra-headed sovereigns that govern contemporary life.

What is left out of Crouch's account is as important as what is left in, which is the sense that citizens are beginning to see themselves as actors in their own right as opposed to that element which is passively spoken for, represented and acted upon in the classic image of representation. The rules are changing. 'The People' is no longer – or much less – an entity that can be spoken for without reproach or challenge. 'Speaking for' becomes problematic as people grow to resent the gesture of being represented and find a way of making *themselves* heard, whether as discrete citizens or as members of NGOs, lobbying groups, online petitionists, agitators, activists, bloggers, critics. It is not democracy that is dying, but rather the image of democracy as an orderly rotation of well-meaning elites motivated by the public interest and the common good. It's an image Crouch speaks to directly in his evocation of the 'good' social democratic elites of the post-war period, as opposed to the 'bad' elites of the neoliberal one. In its place is emerging a more unruly and unpredictable form of politics that offers a challenge to accounts focusing on elites, governments, the state. Should we be concerned, afraid, aghast?

One irony in the evocation of democracy as unpredictable, noisy, unruly, is, as Jacques Rancière notes, that it was precisely these qualities that in Ancient Athens were regarded as intrinsic to democracy (Rancière 2010). Disagreement or dissensus was the stuff of *le politique* or democratic politics. Consensus was, by contrast, associated with authoritarian regimes, tyrannies, regimes where people cowered for fear that their opinions would cost them their lives. Where did the elite-driven politics of the representatives come from? It was, according to Rancière, Manin and others, the product of transforming politics into a technical matter and thus one for experts, not 'anyone and everyone'. Through this switch of emphasis democracy came to be equated with consensus, quiescence and the activity of often distant elites exercising power on our behalf, in our interests and in our name.

The provocative thought prompted by Rancière's account is whether, rather than seeing the emergence of a rather raucous and disorderly politics as representing the death of democracy, we ought to read it as its opposite: the reassertion of the democratic component of democracy from its elite-induced slumber. This is not, and on this reading could not be, equivalent to the *demos* 'taking over', to the People sitting in permanent session to govern itself in the manner sometimes portrayed in accounts of the Athenian *polis*. What it implies, rather, is the emergence of citizens as active components in the democratic process as opposed to that part which is spoken for and which is therefore passive or *pacified* in relation to larger political and economic processes. We can see the nature of this dynamic at work in the increasingly frequent events that have as their object the assertion of the primacy of the *demos* over elites. In certain contexts, such as most recently in Spain, Greece, Iceland, Turkey, Thailand,

Brazil, Hong Kong, we can come to form the impression that politics is being reclaimed by citizens *from* representatives – a kind of insurrection against the political class, or 'democracy versus the state', to paraphrase Miguel Abensour (2011). These are for the present sporadic events. They come and they go in the manner of the evanescent styles of politics we have been documenting. They give witness to deep frustration at one level, but also an appetite for something more participatory and 'public' – more democratic. The scepticism evinced on these occasions is matched by the desire to *democratize* arrangements: to insert a missing dimension, which is the engagement of the *demos* itself in democracy, to reclaim politics back from 'globalization', the EU, finance capitalism, a local authoritarian leader, representatives of whatever stripe. The more democracy takes on the nature of a 'crisis', the more this becomes witness at one level to the underlying dynamic of the age: the exhaustion of representation, on the one hand, and the proliferation of *demoi*, on the other. If post-representative democracy evokes a sense of a *return* of politics, of noise and clamour, then we should at least be reassured that democracy is far from dead. Perhaps at another level it *has only just begun*?

Conclusion

So is it really the end of representative politics? It's the end of the paradigm, the 'metanarrative'. Much of the enthusiasm has gone for the classical model of representative politics and all the paraphernalia that went with it: a belief in the essentially benevolent or well-intentioned motives of those who would represent; a belief that our deepest needs and interests are best off in some other person's hands than our own; a belief that joining a traditional mass party will prove the best use of our time and energies as engaged citizens. The props fall away; but the superstructure is still intact.

What we are left with once the gloss and ideology are stripped back is less than edifying. Notwithstanding the positive story about the myriad ways in which citizens can be and are engaged in politics, the reality is that the world remains intransigently and determinedly replete with injustice, inequality, poverty, exclusion. Politics as the 'small p' business of citizens' initiatives might be buzzing away, but the 'large P' politics of inequality, injustice, ever-concentrating wealth, power and privilege in the hands of the few remains unchanged. In many respects it is getting worse. Might it be that these two facts are inter-linked? Might it be that the greatest threat to the interests, well-being and needs of ordinary citizens is precisely the ebbing of faith or belief in the redeeming power of 'large P' politics – the politics associated with powerful mass parties, whether they be social democratic, socialist or indeed communist? What is there to celebrate in the 'end of representative politics?'

It's a good question. The answer is very little, according to a variety of expert witnesses to what is going on. Crouch, Bauman, Hay, and many others lament the death of social democracy, of organized labour, trade unions and labour parties as the anchor for the welfare state, which in turn delivered housing, health, education, to many who would never otherwise have received them. Žižek, Badiou and Dean lament the unwillingness of many on the left to embrace communism, proxy for a militant politics that is unafraid to name global capitalism as the source of misery and thus as the necessary object for any politics that takes seriously the need to address inequality and injustice. And these are just some of the more high-profile stances against 'the end of representative politics'.

Those who have made it this far will notice that I have tried to resist the mood of nostalgia embracing political commentary of whatever stripe when it comes to considering the fate of representative politics, political parties, ideologies. I see little reason to give that up when confronted directly with the normative and political dimensions of the analysis presented. Looking at the matter squarely, social democracy has not declined for lack of social democratic *parties*. Virtually every political system in the world features a social democratic party or parties. They are in decline not merely because they are failing to connect to their natural constituency, the working class and poorer elements in society, but because many of them have warmly embraced the ideology of market fundamentalism, which we are now asked to consider in terms of the overall picture. As Hay and others lament, it was the UK Labour Party that glorified the City, financialization, outsourcing, the New Public Management and further privatizations. It was the Spanish Social Democrats (PSOE) who backed Spanish banks to pour speculative loans into mega-building projects and investment properties and then backed those banks to recoup bad debts by throwing people out of their homes onto the street. It was the US Democrats who presided over the bailing out of the insurance and finance industries whose reckless investments led to recession and unemployment, and all to the detriment of ordinary taxpayers. One could go on. Social democratic parties have arguably been their own worst enemy when it comes to resisting the decline in the allure of social democracy and the 'large P' politics of creating jobs, protecting public services, supporting the poorest elements in society. Many of today's protests and demonstrations are in reaction to a politics of austerity, on the one hand, and the corruption and cronyism endemic in the political class in many parts of the world, on the other. Social democratic parties have often been implicated in both and become the object of this ire, and rightly so.

A rather different puzzle is provoked by those who insist that we return to communism or neo-communism as a recipe for the ills that confront humanity. They write as if it were possible to 'purge' the term of its connotations with the dreadful inhumanities perpetrated by parties and regimes that have called themselves 'communist'. I don't think it is. If one wants an insight into why, for example, Occupy has the character it has, why participants in today's protests want little to do with 'the Party', with intellectual vanguards and all the rest, then it is the manner in which communism resonates with activists that should offer clues. Initiatives and events like these are not only anti-capitalist, they are *anti-Leninist*, in the sense of self-consciously disavowing the legacy of a form of representative politics that quickly subsided into 'substitutionism', code for the displacement of the self-activity of the working class by a small element of the Party leadership. Communism turned out to be a quintessentially representative discourse and representative form of politics – notwithstanding Marx's insistence that 'the emancipation of the working class must be the act of the working class itself' (Marx 1988: 48). Unfortunately Marx is remembered less for his call for the working class to take control of its own destiny and more for his invitation to see the Communist Party as leading the class and thus as that element that inevitably comes to represent it.

There is a view that many of today's protests and citizens' initiatives take the form they do because of the technological means available, which makes it much easier to construct headless or leaderless movements. This is certainly part of the story, but not the whole part. A key reason is the desire of activists and others to avoid the exclusionary and elitist practices of previous generations, previous movements and initiatives. It is their determination to provide the basis for an inclusionary, participatory and deliberative form of politics that queries and rejects the inheritances of both mainstream and radical political practices, neither of which were able to maintain the necessary trust and confidence of ordinary citizens to avoid decline.

It is early days in this new phase of political mobilization to judge whether and to what extent these newer styles of politics will engage with and be engaging for the poorest elements of society. It is even earlier to judge what their impact might be in terms of governance, and beyond that in terms of policies designed to improve their lot. Recent initiatives suggest that even the most horizontal of activists now see that under representative or post-representative conditions the 'horizontal' may need to be combined with the 'vertical' to leverage alternatives for citizens during elections, to provide a focus for specific campaigns and demands. Beppe Grillo's 5SM, *Podemos*, *Syriza*, various coalitions and blocs have emerged to try to provide a means whereby the unruly 'outside' can find voice and influence within the system of governance itself. Isn't this just 'old wine in new bottles', old leftists in new funky garb designed to embrace the young, the social media folk, the disaffiliated?

Perhaps. But the tune has changed. The expectations have shifted. The recognition of the need to leave behind the mass membership party model, to open the doors to 'Everybody', suggests a recognition of the need to acknowledge that the old models of representation are redundant. So too does the careful choreography around leadership and the avoidance of creating a new cast of 'politicians' for a new 'left populism'. Workers' wages for Euro MPs (*Podemos*); a leader figure (Grillo) who refuses to stand for election; the self-conscious desire to connect and be seen to connect – these all indicate a certain desire to remain loyal to the 'horizontal', participatory, connective energies that brought them into being. But they also indicate a realization that no matter how much state sovereignty has been denuded, there is useful work to be done using the tools the state provides. This includes seeking to roll back some of the worst effects of financialization, outsourcing, environmental degradation, unemployment, precarity, in order to promote the material needs and interests of ordinary citizens. But it is also to open up the system of representation and beyond that the system of governance itself to greater engagement and participation *by* ordinary citizens – the key demand of ¡*Democracia Real YA!*, and of so many of the initiatives we have been documenting. Why *real* democracy? Quite simply because the democracy of the representatives has come to be regarded by many as not only a rather pale imitation of the real thing, but a mechanism for *preventing* ordinary citizens exercising greater control over their own lives. This, to recall Lincoln and many others, was regarded as the true vocation of democracy and the measure by which to judge its success or failure.

NOTES

CHAPTER 1 CONTOURS OF A 'CRISIS'

1 A handy summary of many of the slogans used by the Zapatistas appears here: *http://www.leadershiplearning.org/system/files/Some%20Zapatista%20Prin ciples%20%2526%20Practices.pdf.*

CHAPTER 2 LOCATING 'REPRESENTATIVE POLITICS'

1 For a selection see: *http://www.soane.org/collections_legacy/the_soane_hog arths/an_election.*

CHAPTER 3 ARE WE BECOMING UNREPRESENTABLE?

1 Respectively the titles of the American Political Science Association Annual Conference, 2012, and the UK Political Studies Conference, 2013.
2 *http://www.bbc.co.uk/news/magazine-24079227.*
3 *http://ec.europa.eu/public_opinion/index_en.htm.*
4 *https://www.getup.org.au/.*
5 *http://www.avaaz.org/en/.*
6 *http://www.bbc.co.uk/news/uk-22007058.*

CHAPTER 4 IS THE PARTY OVER?

1 *http://www.resist.org.uk/.*
2 *http://www.theguardian.com/uk/2011/feb/10/uk-uncut-tax-avoidance-twit ter.*
3 *http://www.theguardian.com/world/the-nsa-files.*

CHAPTER 5 CITIZENS AGAINST REPRESENTATION

1 The case study is based on fieldwork carried out in April and June 2013 with Dr Ramón Feenstra of the University Jaume I, Castellón. It consisted of semi-structured interviews, individual and group discussions with approximately a hundred activists and academics in Valencia, Barcelona and Castellón and field visits to numerous organizations, including the regional centres of PAH, ATTAC and *Iai@asflautas*. We attended events including meetings of the Castellón Assembly, the *Iai@asflautas* street festival and the School of the *Indignados*. The websites, social media output and written declarations and programmes of the parties mentioned have also proved invaluable in terms of understanding the structure, motivation and goals of the new political parties.
2 *http://www.usatoday.com/story/news/world/2013/05/08/spanish-monarchy/2145149/*.
3 *http://afectadosporlahipoteca.com/*.
4 *http://www.youtube.com/watch?v=LtNBnc6khHg*.
5 *http://www.presseurop.eu/en/content/news-brief/3858061-european-citizen-s-prize-doesn-t-please-everyone*.
6 *http://www.iaioflautas.org/*.
7 *http://bancexpropiatgracia.wordpress.com/*.
8 *http://www.juntaelectoralcentral.es/portal/page/portal/ JuntaElectoralCentral/JuntaElectoralCentral*.
9 *https://escanos.org/*.
10 *http://partidox.org/en/*.
11 *http://partidox.org/programa/*.
12 *http://cup.cat/*.
13 *http://www.procesconstituent.cat/ca/*.
14 *http://cli-as.org/*.
15 *http://partidoequo.es/*.
16 *http://www.izquierda-unida.es/*.
17 *http://partidodeinternet.es/*; *http://confluyentes.wordpress.com/*; *http://partidopirata.org/*.
18 *http://liquidfeedback.org/*.

CHAPTER 6 DEMOCRACY AFTER REPRESENTATION

1 For other works that explore the idea of resonance as a facet of contemporary politics, see, for example, Invisible Committee 2008; Badiou 2012; Mason 2012.
2 *https://www.youtube.com/watch?v=JGwMIlpgR2A*.
3 *http://play.sydneyoperahouse.com/index.php/media/1491-slavoj-_i_ek-the-impossible-communism.html*.

151

REFERENCES

Abensour, M. (2011) *Democracy against the State: Marx and the Machiavellian Moment*. Cambridge: Polity.

Alcoff, L. (1991) The problem of speaking for others. *Cultural Critique* 20: 5–32.

Amin, A. (2004) Regions unbound: Towards a new politics of place. *Geografiska Annaler: Series B, Human Geography* 86 (1): 33–44.

Anderson, B. (2006) *Imagined Communities: Reflections on the Origin and Spread of Nationalism*. London: Verso.

Anderson, J. (2004) Spatial politics in practice: The style and substance of environmental direct action. *Antipode* 36 (1): 106–25.

Andronikidou, A. and I. Kovras (2012) Cultures of rioting and anti-systemic politics in Southern Europe. *West European Politics* 35 (4): 707–25.

Ankersmit, F. R. (2002) On the origin, nature and future of representative democracy. In *Political Representation*. Stanford: Stanford University Press.

Anon (2010) The party's (largely) over. *The Economist*, 21 October.

Appadurai, A. (1996) *Modernity at Large: Cultural Dimesions of Globalization*. Minneapolis: University of Minnesota Press.

Arquilla, J. and D. Ronfeldt (2000) Swarming and the future of conflict. *http:// www.rand.org/publications/DB/DB311/*.

Badiou, A. (2008) The communist hypothesis. *New Left Review* 49: 29–42.

Badiou, A. (2012) *The Rebirth of History: Times of Riots and Uprisings*. London: Verso.

Bang, H. (2004) Culture governance: Governing self-reflexive modernity. *Public Administration* 82 (1): 157–90.

Bauman, Z. (1987) *Legislators and Interpreters: On Modernity, Post-Modernity, and Intellectuals*. Cambridge: Polity.

Bauman, Z. (1998) *Globalization: The Human Consequences*. Cambridge: Polity.

Bauman, Z. (1999) *In Search of Politics*. Cambridge: Polity.

Bauman, Z. (2001) *The Individualized Society*. Cambridge: Polity.

Bayly, C. A. (2004) *The Birth of the Modern World, 1780–1914: Global Connections and Comparisons*. Oxford: Blackwell.

Beck, U. (1997) *The Reinvention of Politics: Rethinking Modernity in the Global Social Order*. Cambridge: Polity.

REFERENCES

Beck, U. (1992) *Risk Society: Towards a New Modernity*. London: Sage.
Bell, D. (1960) *The End of Ideology*. Cambridge, MA: Harvard University Press.
Bennett, L. and A. Segerberg (2012) The logic of connective action. *Information, Communication & Society* 15 (5): 739–68.
Bennett, S. E. (1998) Young Americans' indifference to media coverage of public affairs. *PS: Political Science and Politics* 31 (3): 535–41.
Bhabha, H. (1994) *The Location of Culture*. London: Routledge.
Bordignon, F. and L. Ceccarini (2013) Five stars and a cricket: Beppe Grillo shakes Italian politics. *South European Society and Politics* 18 (4): 1–23.
Brito Vieira, M. and D. Runciman. (2008) *Representation*. Cambridge: Polity.
Brooke, H. (2012) *The Revolution Will Be Digitised: Dispatches from the Information War*. London: Random House.
Burbach, R. (2001) *Globalization and Postmodern Politics: From Zapatistas to High-Tech Robber Barons*. London: Pluto.
Burchell, D. and A. Leigh (2002) *The Prince's New Clothes: Why Do Australians Dislike Their Politicians?* Sydney: UNSW Press.
Burn-Murdoch, J. (2012) Datablog: 2012 Democratic Audit. *Guardian*, 7 July.
Burn-Murdoch, J. and S. Rogers (2012) UK Election historic turnouts since 1918. *Guardian*, 16 November.
Castañeda, E. (2012) The *Indignados* of Spain: A precedent to Occupy Wall Street. *Social Movement Studies* 11 (3–4): 309–19.
Castells, M. (2012) *Networks of Outrage and Hope: Social Movements in the Internet Age*. Cambridge: Polity.
Charnock, G., T. Purcell and R. Ribera-Fumaz (2011) ¡Indígnate!: The 2011 popular protest and the limits to democracy in Spain. *Capital & Class* 31: 3–11.
Chayes, A. and A. H. Chayes (1998) *The New Sovereignty*. Cambridge, MA: Harvard University Press.
Corner, J. and D. Pels (2003) *Media and the Restyling of Politics: Consumerism, Celebrity and Cynicism*. London: Sage.
Cox, G.W. (1997) *Making Votes Count: Strategic Coordination in the World's Electoral Systems*. Cambridge: Cambridge University Press.
Crouch, C. (2004) *Post-Democracy*. Cambridge: Polity.
Dalton, R. J. (2002) *Citizen Politics: Public Opinion and Political Parties in Advanced Industrial Democracies*. London: Chatham House Publishers.
Dalton, R. J. (2004) *Democratic Challenges, Democratic Choices: The Erosion of Political Support in Advanced Industrial Democracies*. Oxford: Oxford University Press.
Day, R. (2004) From hegemony to affinity: The political logic of the newest social movements. *Cultural Studies* 18 (5): 716–48.
Dean, J. (2009) *Democracy and Other Neoliberal Fantasies: Communicative Capitalism & Left Politics*. Durham, NC: Duke University Press.
Della Porta, D. (2013) *Can Democracy Be Saved? Participation, Deliberation and Social Movements*. Cambridge: Polity.
Della Porta, D. and M. Diani (1998) *Social Movements: An Introduction*. Oxford: Blackwell.
Diani, M. and R. Eyerman (1992) *Studying Collective Action*. London: Sage.
Disch, L. (2011) Toward a mobilization conception of democratic representation. *American Political Science Review* 105 (1): 100–14.

153

Duffield, M. (2007) *Development, Security and Unending War: Governing the World of Peoples*. Cambridge: Polity.

Duverger, M. (1959) *Political Parties*. London: Methuen.

Farrell, D. (1997) *Comparing Electoral Systems*. London: Harvester.

Fisher, W. F. and T. Ponniah (2003) *Another World Is Possible: Popular Alternatives to Globalization at the World Social Forum*. London and New York: Zed Books.

Fleras, A. and J. L. Elliott (1992) *The Nations Within: Aboriginal–State Relations in Canada, the United States, and New Zealand*. Cambridge: Cambridge University Press.

Flinders, M. (2012) *Defending Politics: Why Democracy Matters in the Twenty-First Century*. Oxford: Oxford University Press.

FnfEurope (2013) The Spanish slump – political crisis and the need for institutional reform. *http://fnf-europe.org/2013/06/17/the-spanish-slump-political-crisis-and-the-need-for-institutional-reform/*.

Foot, P. (2005) *The Vote: How It Was Won and How It Was Undermined*. London: Penguin.

Foucault, M. (1980) *Power/Knowledge: Selected Interviews and Other Writings, 1972–1977*. London: Random House.

Freeman, J. (2013) The tyranny of structurelessness. *WSQ: Women's Studies Quarterly* 41 (3): 231–46.

Fukuyama, F. (1992) *The End of History and the Last Man*. London: Penguin.

Fuster Morell, M. (2012) The free culture and 15M movements in Spain: Composition, social networks and synergies. *Social Movement Studies* 11 (3–4): 386–91.

Gallagher, M. and P. Mitchell (2005) *The Politics of Electoral Systems*. Cambridge: Cambridge University Press.

Gautney, H. (2012) *Protest and Organization in the Alternative Globalization Era: NGOs, Social Movements, and Political Parties*. London: Palgrave Macmillan.

Genosko, G. (2003) *The Party without Bosses*. Manitoba, CA: ARP.

Giddens, A. (1991) *Modernity and Self-Identity: Self and Society in the Late Modern Age*. Stanford, CA: Stanford University Press.

Giroux, H. A. (2011) *Zombie Politics and Culture in the Age of Casino Capitalism*. New York: Peter Lang.

Gladwell, M. (2010) Small change: Why the revolution will not be tweeted. *The New Yorker*, 4 October.

Godwin, W. (2013) *An Enquiry Concerning Political Justice*. Oxford: Oxford University Press.

Goleman, D. (2006) *Emotional Intelligence: Why It Can Matter More Than IQ*. New York: Random House.

Goot, M. (2002) Distrustful, disenchanted and disengaged? Polled opinion on politics, politicians and the parties: An historical perspective. *Parliament and Public Opinion, Papers on Parliament* 38: 17–58.

Granger, S. (2013) Quikstats: Australian political party membership. *http://gmggranger.wordpress.com/2013/10/15/quikstats-australian-political-party-membership/*.

Hardt, M. and A. Negri (2004) *Multitude: War and Democracy in the Age of Empire*. New York: Penguin.

Hardt, M. and A. Negri (2009) *Empire*. Cambridge, MA: Harvard University Press.

Harvey, D. (1989) *The Condition of Postmodernity*. Oxford: Blackwell.

Hay, C. (2007) *Why We Hate Politics*. Cambridge: Polity.

Hayward, J. (ed.) (1996). *The Crisis of Representation in Europe*. Abingdon, Oxon: Routledge.

Heller, A. (1990) *A Philosophy of Morals*. Oxford: Basil Blackwell.

Heller, A. (1999). The postmodern imagination. In C. Pierson and S. Tormey (eds) *Politics at the Edge: The PSA Yearbook 1999*. London: Palgrave.

Heller, A. and F. Feher (1988) *The Postmodern Political Condition*. Cambridge: Polity.

Hessel, S. (2011). *Indignez-vous!* (bilingual edn). Melbourne: Scribe.

Hewitt, V. (2007). *Political Mobilisation and Democracy in India: States of Emergency*. London: Routledge.

Heywood, P. and J. Grugel (1995). *The Government and Politics of Spain*. Cambridge: Cambridge University Press.

Heywood, P. and I. Krastev (2006). Political scandals and corruption. In P. Heywood, E. Jones, M. Rhodes and U. Sedelmeier (eds) *Developments in European Politics*. Baskingstoke: Palgrave.

Hill, C. (1972) *The World Turned Upside Down: Radical Ideas during the English Revolution*. London: Penguin.

Hill, S. (2013). *Digital Revolutions: Activism in the Internet Age*. Oxford: New Internationalist.

Holliday, I., D. Farrell and P. Webb (2002) *Political Parties in Advanced Industrial Democracies*. Oxford: Oxford University Press.

Holloway, J. (2002) *Change the World without Taking Power*. London: Pluto.

Holloway, J. and E. Pelaez (eds) (1998) *Zapatista! Reinventing Revolution in Mexico*. London: Pluto.

Hughes, N. (2011) Young people took to the streets and all of a sudden all of the political parties got old: The 15M movement in Spain. *Social Movement Studies* 10 (4): 407–13.

Humphrey, R. H. (2002) The many faces of emotional leadership. *The Leadership Quarterly* 13 (5): 493–504.

Inglehart, R. (1990) *Culture Shift in Advanced Industrial Society*. Princeton, NJ: Princeton University Press.

Invisible Committee (2008) *The Coming Insurrection*. New York: Semiotext(e).

Jessop, R. (1982) *The Capitalist State: Marxist Theories and Methods*. Oxford: Basil Blackwell.

Kaldor, M., S. Selchow, S. Deel and T. Murray-Leach (2012) The 'bubbling up' of subterranean politics in Europe. LSE Project Report, London. *http://eprints. lse.ac.uk/44873*.

Katzenberger, E. (1995) *First World, Ha Ha Ha! The Zapatista Challenge*. San Francisco: City Lights Books.

Keane, J. (2009) *The Life and Death of Democracy*. London and New York: Simon & Schuster.

Keane, J. (2011) Monitory democracy? In S. Alonso, J. Keane and W. Merkel (eds) *The Future of Representatative Democracy*. Cambridge: Cambridge University Press.

Kuhn, T. S. (2012) *The Structure of Scientific Revolutions*. Chicago: University of Chicago Press.

REFERENCES

Kymlicka, W. (2001) *Politics in the Vernacular: Nationalism, Multiculturalism, and Citizenship*. Oxford: Oxford University Press.

Laclau, E. and C. Mouffe (1985) *Hegemony and Socialist Strategy: Towards a Radical Democratic Politics*. London: Verso.

Lasswell, H. (1936) *Politics: Who Gets What, When, How*. New York: McGraw-Hill.

Lawson, K. (2010) *Political Parties and Democracy*. Santa Barbara, CA: Praeger.

Livingstone, K. (1987) *If Voting Changed Anything, They'd Abolish It*. London: Collins.

Lyotard, J.-F. (1984) *The Postmodern Condition: A Report on Knowledge*. Manchester: Manchester University Press.

McGrew, A. and P. Lewis (2013) *Global Politics: Globalization and the Nation-State*. London: John Wiley & Sons.

McKinley, J. (2005) At a 60s style be-in, guns yield to words, lots of words. *The New York Times*, 31 August.

Macpherson, C. B. (1962) *The Political Theory of Possessive Individualism: Hobbes to Locke*. Oxford: Oxford University Press.

Mair, P. and I. Van Biezen (2001) Party membership in twenty European democracies, 1980–2000. *Party Politics* 7 (1): 5–21.

Manin, B. (1997) *The Principles of Representative Government*. Cambridge: Cambridge University Press.

Mansbridge, J. (2003) Rethinking representation. *American Political Science Review* 97 (4): 515–28.

Marcos, Subcomandante Insurgente (2003) I shit on all the revolutionary vanguards of this planet. *http://flag.blackened.net/revolt/mexico/ezln/2003/marcos/etaJAN.html*.

Marcuse, H. (1964) *One Dimensional Man*. London: Sphere Books.

Markus, A. (2013) *Mapping Social Cohesion*. Scanlon Foundation, Monash University, Melbourne. *http://scanlonfoundation.org.au/wp-content / uploads / 2014 / 07 / mapping - social - cohesion - national-report-2013.pdf*.

Markusen, A. R. (1987) *Regions: The Economics and Politics of Territory*. Totowa, NJ: Rowman & Littlefield.

Marx, K. (1976) *Capital*. London: Penguin.

Marx, K. (1988) *The Communist Manifesto*. London: Norton.

Marx, K. (1996) The civil war in France. In *Marx: Later Political Writings* (ed. T. Carver). Cambridge: Cambridge University Press.

Mason, P. (2012) *Why It's Kicking Off Everywhere: The New Global Revolutions*. London: Verso.

Mertes, T. and W. F. Bello (2004) *A Movement of Movements: Is Another World Really Possible?* London: Verso.

Meyer, T. and L. P. Hinchman (2002) *Media Democracy: How the Media Colonize Politics*. Cambridge: Polity.

Micheletti, M. (2003) *Political Virtue and Shopping: Individuals, Consumerism and Collective Action*. New York: Palgrave.

Michels, R. (1998) *Political Parties: A Sociological Study of the Oligarchical Tendencies of Modern Democracy*. New York: Transaction.

Micó, J.-L. and A. Casero-Ripollés (2013) Political activism online: Organization and media relations in the case of 15M in Spain. *Information, Communication & Society* 17 (7): 1–14.

Mignolo, W. (2012) *Local Histories/Global Designs: Coloniality, Subaltern*

Knowledges, and Border Thinking. Princeton, NJ: Princeton University Press.

Miliband, R. (1969) *The State in Capitalist Society*. New York: Basic Books.

Mill, J. S. (1972) Considerations on representative government. In *Three Essays*. Oxford: Oxford University Press.

Miller, P. (2010) *The Smart Swarm: How Understanding Flocks, Schools, and Colonies Can Make Us Better at Communicating, Decision Making, and Getting Things Done*. New York: Avery Publishing Group.

Moffitt, B. (2014) How to perform crisis: A model for understanding the key role of crisis in contemporary populism. *Government & Opposition*. DOI: *http://dx.doi.org/10.1017/gov.2014.13*. Published online 29 May.

Moffitt, B. and S. Tormey (2014) Rethinking populism: Politics, mediatisation and political style. *Political Studies* 62 (2): 381–97.

Morozov, E. (2012) *The Net Delusion: The Dark Side of Internet Freedom*. London: Penguin.

Mouffe, C. (1993) *The Return of the Political*. London: Verso.

Newton, K. and P. Norris (2000) Confidence in public institutions. In S. J. Pharr and R. D. Putnam (eds) *Disaffected Democracies: What's Troubling the Trilateral Countries?* Princeton, NJ: Princeton University Press.

Norris, P. (1999) *Critical Citizens: Global Support for Democratic Government*. Oxford: Oxford University Press.

Norris, P. (2002) *Democratic Phoenix: Reinventing Political Activism*. Cambridge: Cambridge University Press.

Norris, P. (2011) *Democratic Deficit*. Cambridge: Cambridge University Press.

Parekh, B. C. (2002) *Rethinking Multiculturalism: Cultural Diversity and Political Theory*. Cambridge, MA: Harvard University Press.

Pickerill, J. (2003) *Cyberprotest: Environmental Activism Online*. Manchester: Manchester University Press.

Pierson, C. (2011) *The Modern State*. London: Routledge.

Piketty, T. (2014) *Capital in the Twenty-First Century*. Cambridge, MA: Harvard University Press.

Pitkin, H. F. (1972) *The Concept of Representation*. Berkeley: University of California Press.

Piven, F. F. and R. A. Cloward (1988) *Poor People's Movements: Why They Succeed, How They Fail*. New York: Random House.

Poggi, G. (1978) *The Development of the Modern State: A Sociological Introduction*. Stanford, CA: Stanford University Press.

Poguntke, T. and P. Webb (2007) *The Presidentialization of Politics: A Comparative Study of Modern Democracies*. Oxford: Oxford University Press.

Posner, R. A. (2009) *Public Intellectuals: A Study of Decline*. Cambridge, MA: Harvard University Press.

Postill, J. (2013) Democracy in an age of viral reality: A media epidemiography of Spain's Indignados movement. *Ethnography* 15: 51-69.

Putnam, R. D. (2000) *Bowling Alone: The Collapse and Revival of American Community*. New York: Touchstone.

Rae, H. (2002) *State Identities and the Homogenisation of Peoples*. Cambridge: Cambridge University Press.

Rancière, J. (2010) *Dissensus: On Politics and Aesthetics*. London: Continuum.

Rehfeld, A. (2009) Representation rethought: On trustees, delegates, and gyroscopes in the study of political representation and democracy. *American Political Science Review* 103 (2): 214–30.

Riddell, P. (2010) In defence of politicians: In spite of themselves. *Parliamentary Affairs* 63 (3): 545–57.

Robinson, A. and S. Tormey (2005) Horizontals, verticals and the conflicting logics of transformative politics. In C. el-Ojeili and P. Hayden (eds) *Confronting Globalization*. London: Palgrave.

Rosanvallon, P. (2002) *Le peuple introuvable: Histoire de la représentation démocratique en France*. Paris: Gallimard.

Rosanvallon, P. (2008) *Counter-Democracy: Politics in an Age of Distrust*. Cambridge: Cambridge University Press.

Rosanvallon, P. (2011) *Democratic Legitimacy: Impartiality, Reflexivity, Proximity*. Princeton, NJ: Princeton University Press.

Rousseau, J.-J. (1985) *The Social Contract*. London: Penguin.

Sartori, G. (2005) *Parties and Party Systems: A Framework for Analysis*. Colchester: ECPR Press.

Sassen, S. (1996) *Losing Control? Sovereignty in an Age of Globalization*. New York: Columbia University Press.

Sassen, S. (2006) *Territory, Authority, Rights: From Medieval to Global Assemblages*. Princeton, NJ: Princeton University Press.

Saward, M. (2010) *The Representative Claim*. Oxford: Oxford University Press.

Saward, M. (2011) The wider canvass: Representation and democracy in state and society. In S. Alonso, J. Keane and W. Merkel (eds) *The Future of Representative Democracy*. Cambridge: Cambridge University Press.

Scott, J. (1987) *Weapons of the Weak: Everyday Forms of Peasant Resistance*. New Haven, CT: Yale University Press.

Sen, J. (ed.) (2004) *World Social Forum: Challenging Empires*. New Delhi: Viveka.

Sen, J. (2007) *A Political Programme for the World Social Forum*. New Delhi: CACIM.

Shirkey, C. (2009) *Here Comes Everybody: The Power of Organizing without Organizations*. New York: Penguin.

Smith, G. (2009) *Democratic Innovations: Designing Institutions for Citizen Participation*. Cambridge: Cambridge University Press.

Soutphommasane, T. (2009) *Reclaiming Patriotism: Nation-Building for Australian Progressives*. Melbourne: Cambridge University Press.

Street, J. (2001) *Mass Media, Politics and Democracy*. Basingstoke: Palgrave.

Sutton, R. (2010) *Good Boss, Bad Boss*. London: Hachette.

Taibo, C. (2013) The Spanish *Indignados*: A movement with two souls. *European Urban and Regional Studies* 20: 155–8.

Talmon, J. L. (1961) *The Origins of Totalitarian Democracy*. London: Mercury Books.

Thomas, J. (2004) *Popular Newspapers, the Labour Party and British Politics*. London: Routledge.

Thompson, J. (2000) *Political Scandal: Power and Visibility in the Media Age*. Cambridge: Polity.

Thompson, P. and D. McHugh (1990) *Work Organisations: A Critical Introduction*. London: Palgrave.

Toret, J. (2013) *Tecnopolítica: La potencia de las multitudes conectadas: El sistema red 15M, un nuevo paradigma de la política.* UOC Distribuida, Barcelona.

Tormey, S. (2004) *Anti-Capitalism: A Beginner's Guide.* Oxford: Oneworld.

Tormey, S. (2006) Not in my name: Deleuze, Zapatismo and the critique of representation. *Parliamentary Affairs* 59 (1): 138–54.

Tormey, S. (2012) Occupy Wall Street: From representation to post-representation. *Journal of Critical Globalisation Studies* 5: 132–7.

Urbinati, N. (2006) *Representative Democracy: Principles and Genealogy.* Chicago: University of Chicago Press.

Urbinati, N. (2011) Representative democracy and its critics. In S. Alonso, J. Keane and W. Merkel (eds) *The Future of Representative Democracy.* Cambridge: Cambridge University Press.

Van Biezen, I. (2004) Political parties as public utilities. *Party Politics* 10 (6): 701–22.

Van Biezen, I., P. Mair and T. Poguntke (2012) Going, going, . . . gone? The decline of party membership in contemporary Europe. *European Journal of Political Research* 51 (1): 24–56.

van de Donk, W., B. D. Loader, P. G. Nixon and D. Rucht (eds) (2004) *Cyberprotest: New Media, Citizens and Social Movements.* London: Routledge.

Wade, R. H. (2011) Emerging world order? From multipolarity to multilateralism in the G20, the World Bank, and the IMF. *Politics & Society* 39 (3): 347–78.

Wark, M. (2011). How to occupy an abstraction. *http://www.versobooks. com/blogs/728-mckenzie-wark-on-occupy-wall-street-how-to-occupy-an-abstraction.*

Wessels, B. (2011) Performance and deficits of present-day representation. In S. Alonso, J. Keane and W. Merkel (eds) *The Future of Representative Democracy.* Cambridge: Cambridge University Press.

Whiteley, P. (2011) Is the party over? The decline of party activism and membership across the democratic world. *Party Politics* 17 (1): 21–44.

Williamson, V., T. Skocpol and J. Coggin (2011) The Tea Party and the remaking of Republican conservatism. *Perspectives on Politics* 9 (1): 25–43.

Wilson, F. (2013) *Organizational Behaviour and Work: A Critical Introduction.* Oxford: Oxford University Press.

Wolin, S. (1996) Fugitive democracy. In S. Benhabib (ed.) *Democracy and Difference: Contesting the Boundaries of the Political.* Princeton, NJ: Princeton University Press.

Zernike, K. (2010) *Boiling Mad: Inside Tea Party America.* London: Macmillan.

Žižek, S. (2002) The fragile absolute: Or, why is the Christian legacy worth fighting for? *Theoria* 99: 141–3.

Žižek, S. (2011) *Living in the End of Times.* London: Verso.

Žižek, S. (2012a) Occupy Wall Street: What is to be done next? *Guardian*, 24 April.

Žižek, S. (2012b) *The Year of Dreaming Dangerously.* London: Verso.

INDEX